LOWRI NICHOLLS
3GH

CW00664582

for Robert Bigio, Steve James and Avril Williams

Sally Adams's

Flute Basics

A method for individual and group learning

PUPIL'S BOOK

Teacher's book: ISBN 0-571-52000-6

with illustrations by Drew Hillier

Accompaniment CD: 0-571-52153-3

contains all the piano and flute accompaniments from the Teacher's book

FABER ff MUSIC

Acknowledgements

I'd like to thank Kathryn Oswald, Paul Harris, Alison Davies, Martin Pye and Joy Adams for all their help and support. Thanks are also due to all my flute students—past, present and future—without whom *Flute Basics* would never have happened.

Sally Adams

Unless stated otherwise, all musical content in the pupil's book is by Sally Adams.

© 2002 by Faber Music Ltd
First published in 2002 by Faber Music Ltd
3 Queen Square London WC1N 3AU
Music processed by Jackie Leigh
Design by Nick Flower
Printed in England by Caligraving Ltd
All rights reserved

ISBN 0-571-52001-4

To buy Faber Music publications or to find out about the full range of titles available please contact your local music retailer or Faber Music sales enquiries:

Faber Music Limited, Burnt Mill, Elizabeth Way, Harlow, CM20 2HX England
Tel: +44 (0)1279 82 89 82   Fax: +44 (0)1279 82 89 83
sales@fabermusic.com   www.fabermusic.com

INTRODUCTION

Welcome to *Flute Basics*!

And welcome to the most popular of all woodwind instruments, the flute. With the help of *Flute Basics* you will soon be playing lots of fun tunes that will impress your family and friends.

To help you on your way, here are some useful hints.

- From the very start ask your teacher or somebody else to play the flute and piano parts from the teacher's book—perhaps get them to record them on to a tape so that you can perform them to your friends.
- Play your flute to anyone who will listen to you (even if it's just the dog!). Playing in front of any audience, large or small, is the best way to become a confident flautist.
- If there is anything you don't understand, ask your teacher to help you.
- Take care of your flute—always clean it after you have played it and put it back in its case.
- Practise as often as you can—remember: 'Practice every day keeps teacher at bay …'
- Listen to lots of different kinds of music—not just flute music.

I hope you have as much fun learning from *Flute Basics* as I did!

Sally Adams

Mistress Adams.
FLUTE TUTORESS

A HEAD START ...

Welcome to
Flute Basics!
Before you put your flute together, have a go at playing all the pieces on these two pages on just the head-joint. Have fun!

semibreve/whole note: **4 beats**

Count: 1 2 3 4 1 2 3 4

semibreve/whole note rest: **4 beats**

Count: 1 2 3 4 1 2 3 4

Twinkle, twinkle little sputnik

Wolfgang Amadeus Mozart

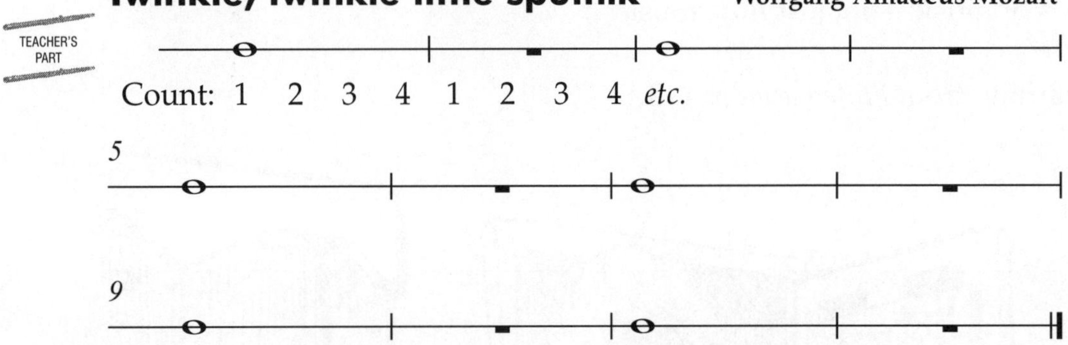
TEACHER'S PART
Count: 1 2 3 4 1 2 3 4 etc.
5
9

Head-joint Harlequin

Say 'TUU—' as you play each note.

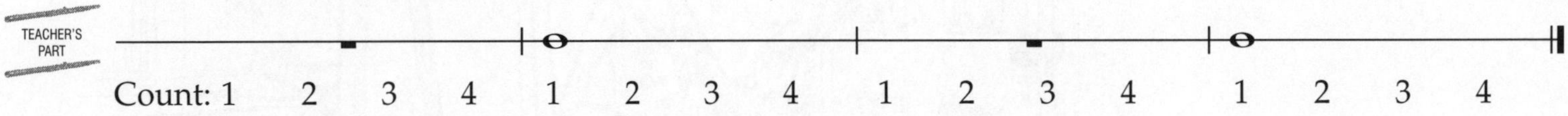
TEACHER'S PART
Count: 1 2 3 4 1 2 3 4 1 2 3 4 1 2 3 4

Head-joint relay (duet)

Pass the note without making a gap in sound. Do your notes all sound the same?

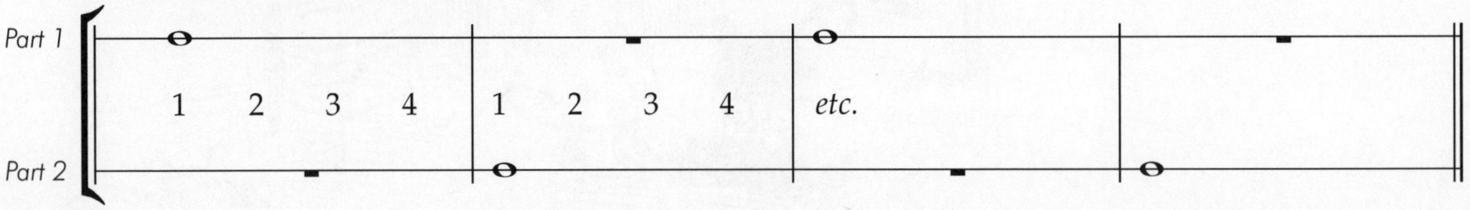
Part 1
1 2 3 4 1 2 3 4 etc.
Part 2

Pavane

Gabriel Fauré

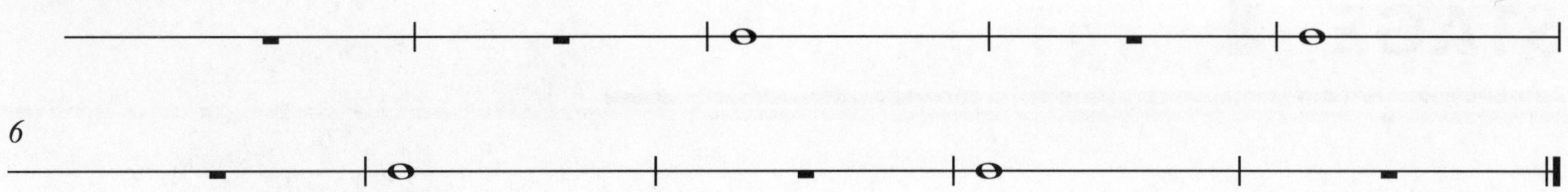

HEAD-JOINT MAGIC

You can make lots of different notes just using the head-joint alone!

① Play a long note on the head-joint: does the note stay the same or does it go higher or lower?

② Try rolling the head-joint towards and away from your mouth and see what happens!

③ Now put your finger in and out of the end of the head-joint while you play, or put the palm of your hand over the end. What happens to the note?

④ Can you play any well-known pieces using these higher and lower sounds?

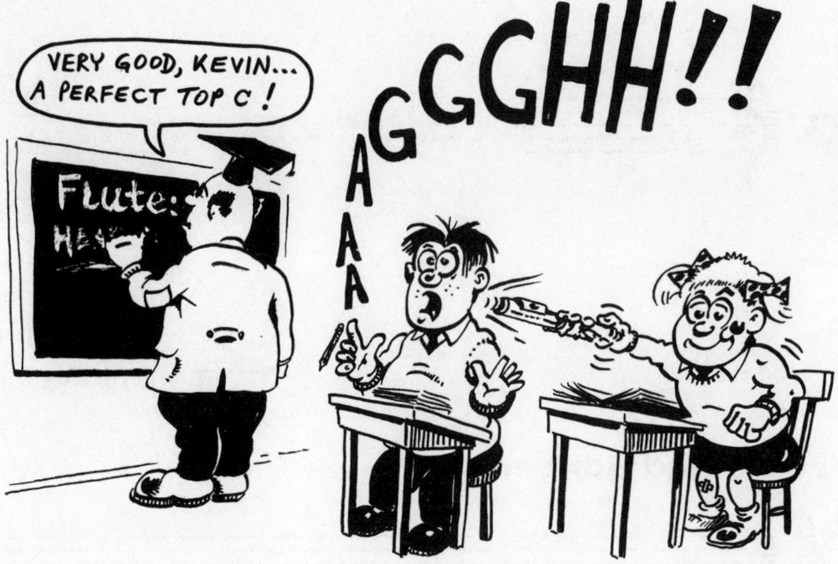
VERY GOOD, KEVIN... A PERFECT TOP C !
Flute:
AAAGGGHH!!

Head-joint Hobo

** Roll the head-joint towards you to make the sound lower.*

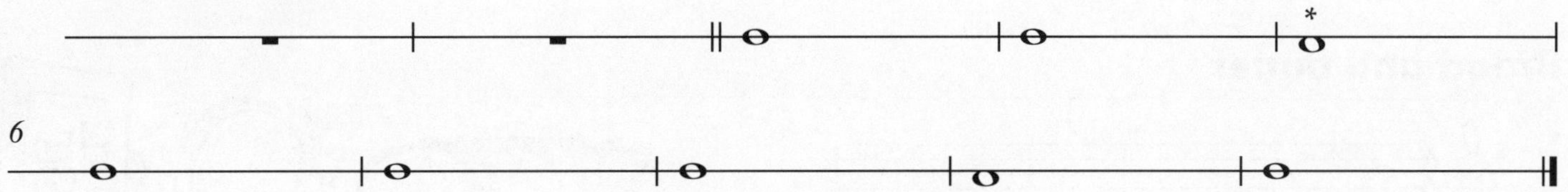

HOT TIP!

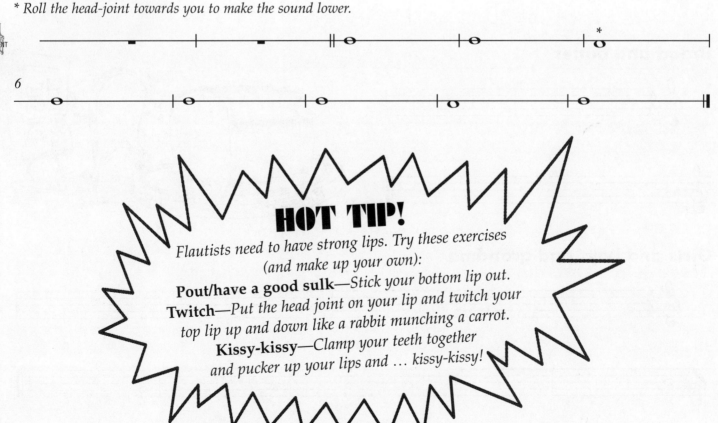

Flautists need to have strong lips. Try these exercises (and make up your own):

Pout/have a good sulk—*Stick your bottom lip out.*

Twitch—*Put the head joint on your lip and twitch your top lip up and down like a rabbit munching a carrot.*

Kissy-kissy—*Clamp your teeth together and pucker up your lips and … kissy-kissy!*

STAGE 1

FACT FILE

Notes are written on a five-lined **stave**.

The symbol 𝄞 at the beginning of each stave is called a **treble clef**.

Music is divided into units of time – **bars** or **measures** – by **barlines**.

A double barline shows the end of a piece.

The **time signature** is the two numbers at the beginning of a piece. The top number tells you how many beats there are in a bar, so $\frac{4}{4}$ means four beats per bar.

B

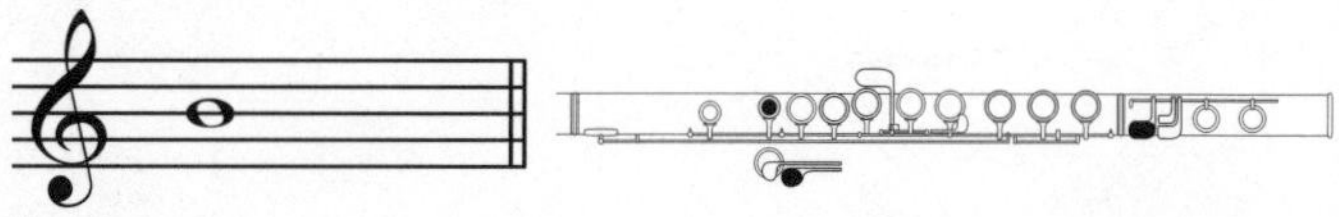

A

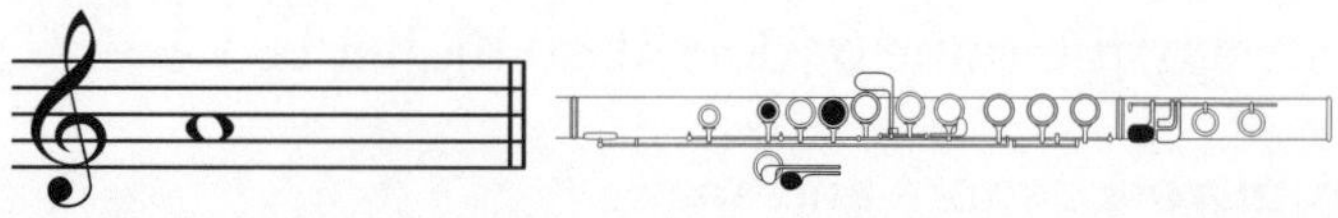

G

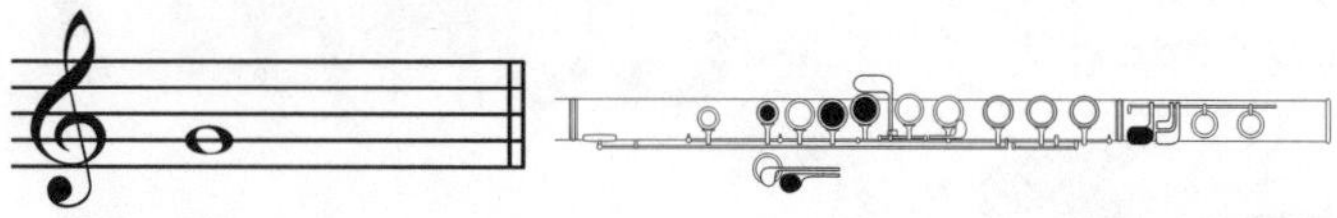

Remember to keep your right-hand little finger down.

Goose and gander

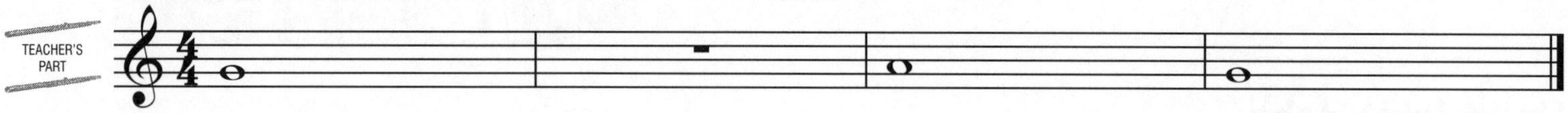
TEACHER'S PART

Bread and butter

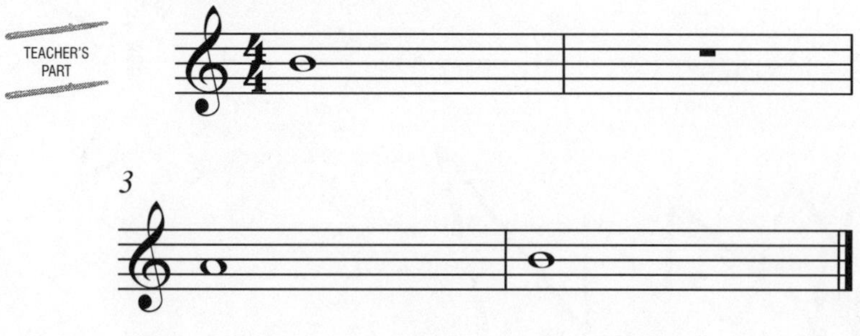
TEACHER'S PART
3

BUTTER DISH
BREAD

Girls and boys and grandma

TEACHER'S PART
5

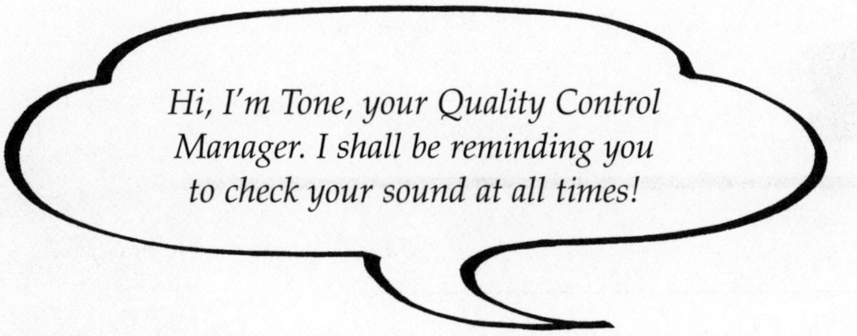
Hi, I'm Tone, your Quality Control Manager. I shall be reminding you to check your sound at all times!

TONE
QUALITY CONTROL MANAGER

Eine kleine Nachtmusik

Wolfgang Amadeus Mozart

Aria

Flowing

HOT TIP!

Use your tongue to start a note on your flute.

Say 'Twen-ty Tur-tles' several times, then play four Gs, thinking the same words ('TUU—TUU—TUU—TUU—'). What has happened to your sound?

Not convinced? Try talking to someone without using your tongue …

¿QUIZ?

① Shut your eyes and get your teacher to say one of the new notes you have learnt: B, A or G. How long does it take you to find the fingering and play it?

② Close your copy of *Flute Basics*, and explain to your teacher what 4/4 means.

③ Make up your own tune using B, A and G. You can either memorize it, or write it down on the following stave. Don't forget to give it a title!

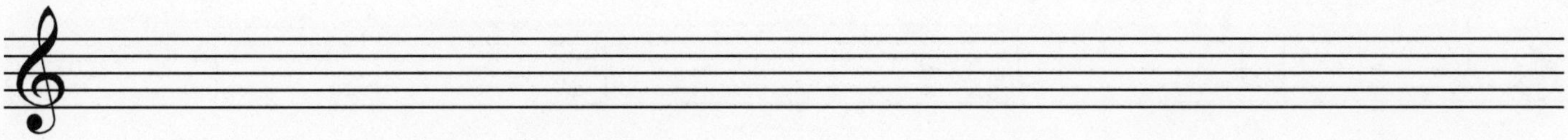

STAGE 2

FACT FILE
Submarine semibreve/whole note rest sits under the water.
Motorboat minim/half note rest sits on top of the water.

𝅗𝅥	**minim/half note:**	**2 beats**
𝄼	**minim/half note rest:**	**2 beats**

Clap: 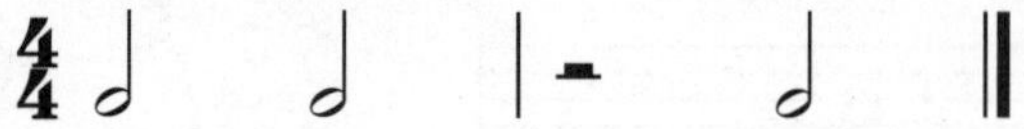

Count: 1 2 3 4 1 2 3 4

IT'S NOT A WIND-UP!
SHEET MUSIC
SHEET MUSIC
DeLuxe™ FLUTE
FLUTE
DeLuxe™ FLUTE

A musical box

You'll have to think about where to breathe—can you play a whole bar in one breath?

Moving

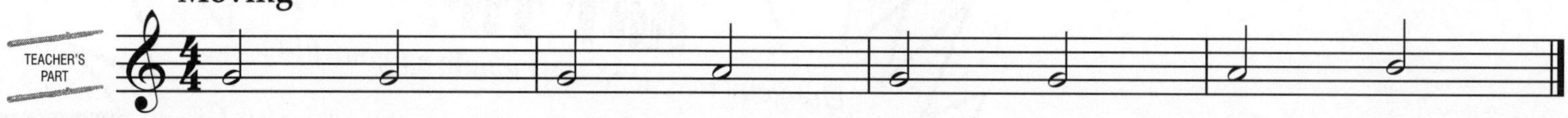
TEACHER'S PART

Hebrew melody

Traditional Hebrew

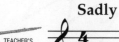

Sadly

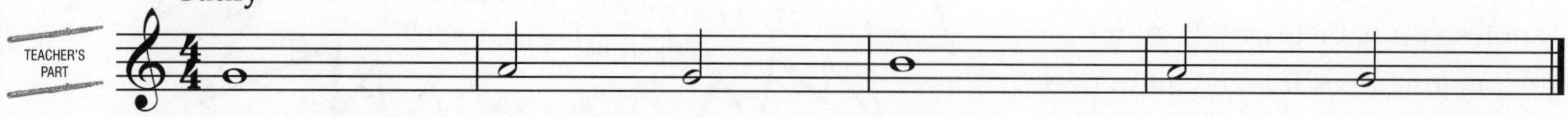
TEACHER'S PART

Midnight tango

PIANO ACCOMPANIMENT
8

Icacato – the sacred lake

Gently
6

Compact chorale

Steadily
8

BREATH TESTS

First, have a big 'YAWN'.

Now breathe out slowly through your mouth and lean forward as you do so.

Then breathe in slowly and pull yourself upright.

Test 1

- Breathe out again, standing still this time.
- Now breathe in quickly with one big gasp as if you have been surprised by something. What happens to your tummy muscles when you do this?

Test 2

- Breathe in for 4 counts—hold for 4 counts—breathe out for 4 counts.
- Breathe in for 2 counts—hold for 4 counts—breathe out for 6 counts.
- Breathe in for 1 count—hold for 6 counts—breathe out for 8 counts.

STAGE 3

FACT FILE

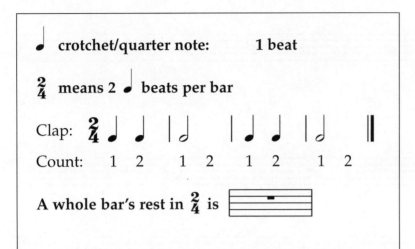

Some *Italian* terms …

Allegro means **quickly.**

Moderato means at a **moderate speed.**

♩ **crotchet/quarter note: 1 beat**

2/4 means 2 ♩ beats per bar

Clap:

Count: 1 2 1 2 1 2 1 2

A whole bar's rest in 2/4 is 

HOT TIP
Your right-hand little finger must be on when you play C; keep it nice and curved.

C 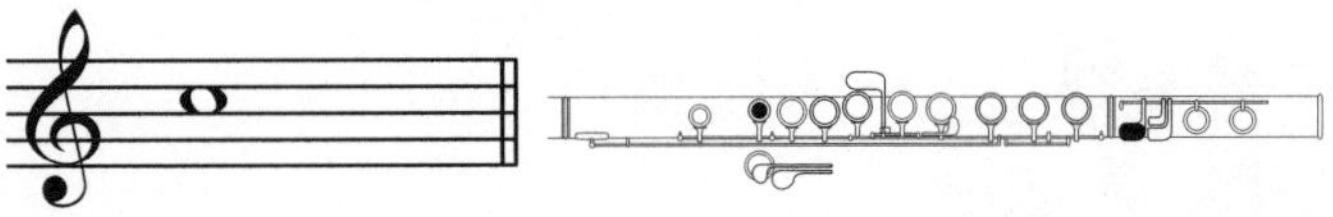

Warm-up

TEACHER'S PART
Twen - ty tur - tles etc.

I like to B by the C

Make sure your flute doesn't wobble when you play from B to C.

TEACHER'S PART
3

C MAJOR
C MINOR

Mysterious madrigal

Mysteriously
PIANO ACCOMPANIMENT

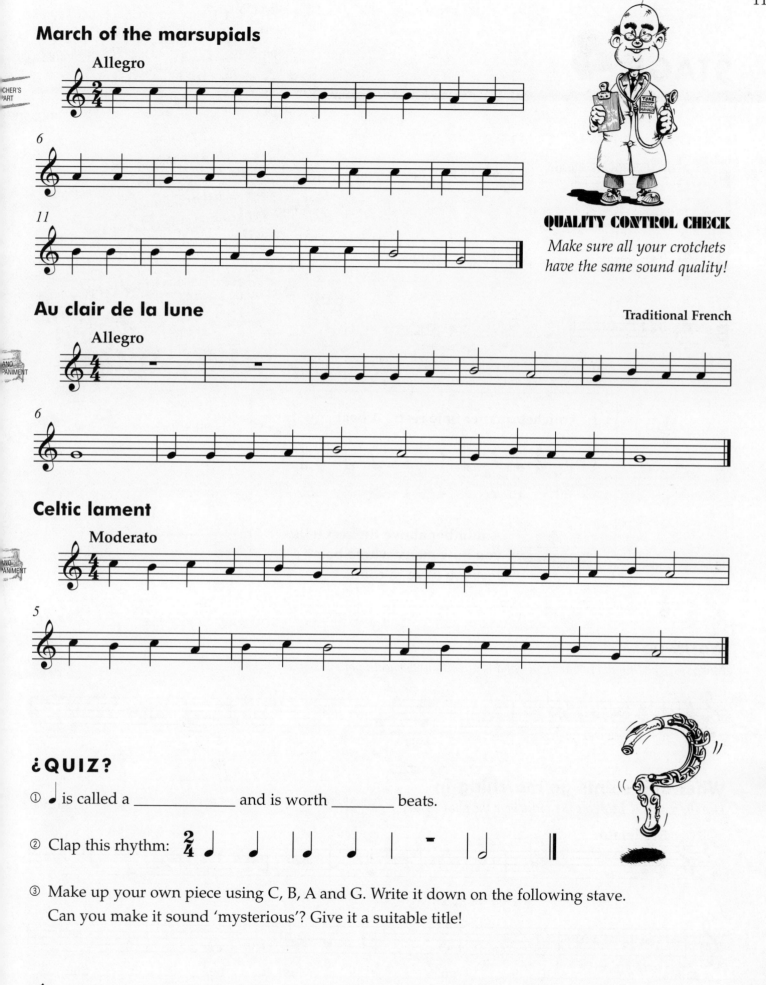

March of the marsupials

Allegro
6
11

TONE QUALITY CONTROL MANAGER

QUALITY CONTROL CHECK

Make sure all your crotchets have the same sound quality!

Au clair de la lune

Traditional French

Allegro
6

Celtic lament

Moderato
5

¿QUIZ?

① ♩ is called a ____________ and is worth ________ beats.

② Clap this rhythm:

③ Make up your own piece using C, B, A and G. Write it down on the following stave.
Can you make it sound 'mysterious'? Give it a suitable title!

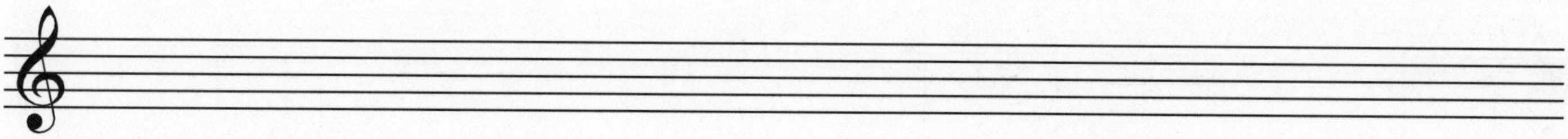

STAGE 4

F

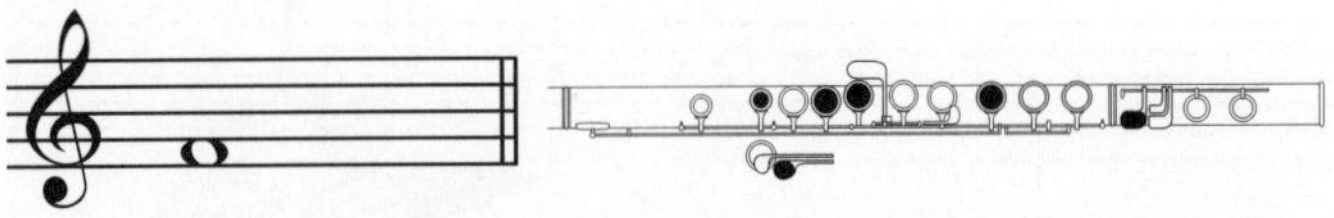

B♭

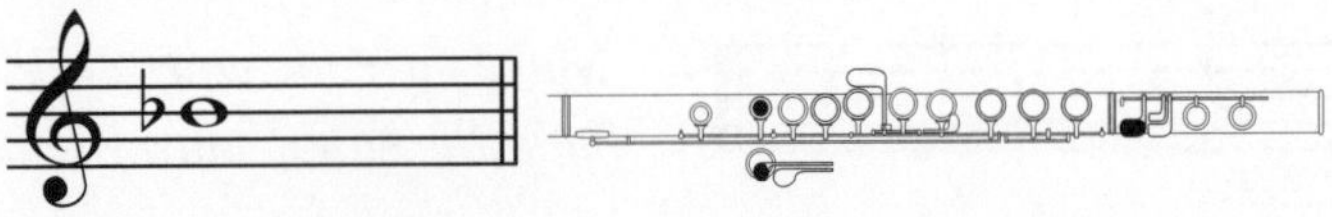

B♭

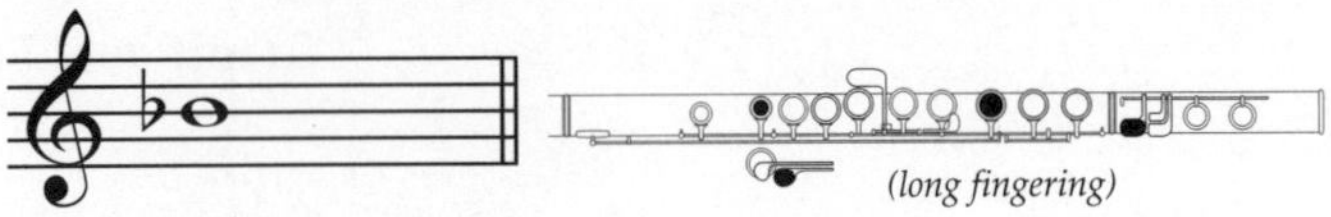
(long fingering)

> **FACT FILE**
>
> A **flat sign** ♭ in front of a note lowers it by a **semitone** ('half a tone').
>
> A flat or sharp sign is cancelled by a **natural sign** ♮.
>
> Flats ♭, naturals ♮ and sharps ♯ (you'll learn about these in Stage 7) occurring within a piece are called **accidentals**.
>
> **Important rule**: accidentals maintain their effect until the end of a bar.
>
> Just as you group words into sentences, music is grouped into **phrases**.

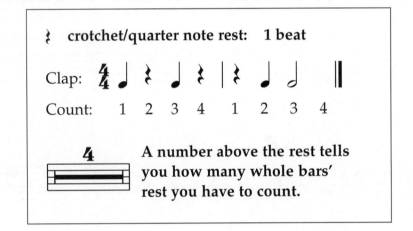

𝄽 crotchet/quarter note rest: 1 beat

Clap:

Count: 1 2 3 4 1 2 3 4

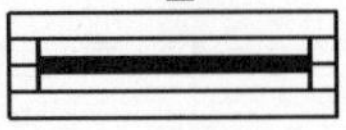
4

A number above the rest tells you how many whole bars' rest you have to count.

Warm-up

Make sure the thumb of your right hand is directly underneath your F key.

TEACHER'S PART

When the saints go marching in

Use the words to help to work out where the phrases are.

Spiritual

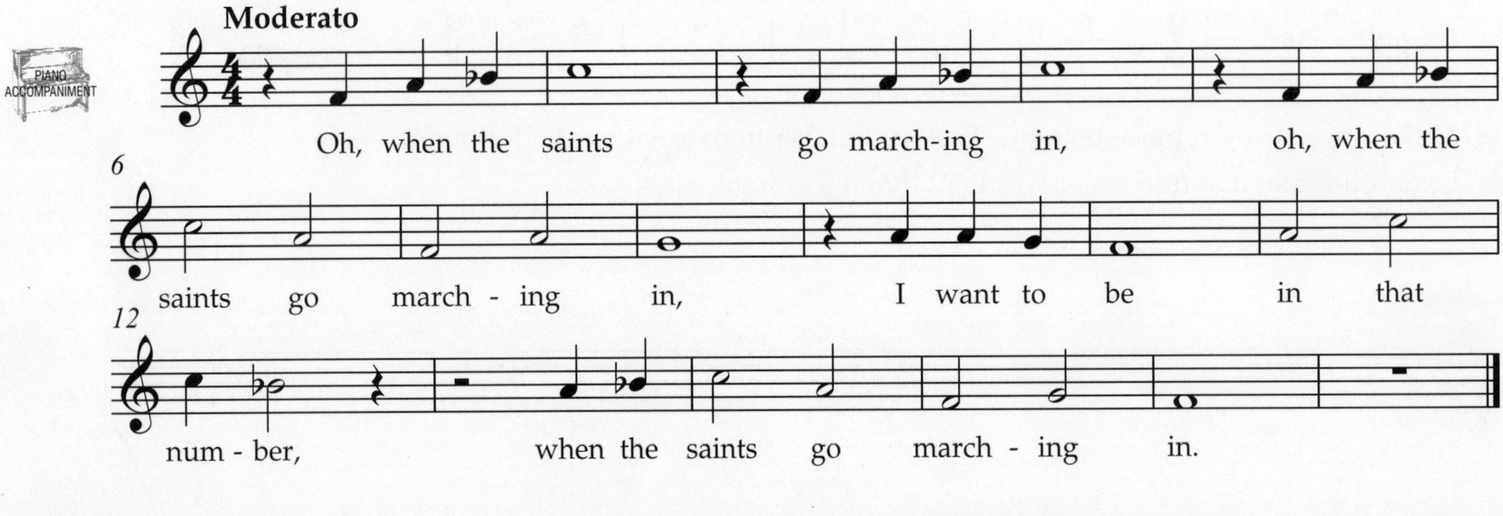
Moderato
PIANO ACCOMPANIMENT
Oh, when the saints go march-ing in, oh, when the
6
saints go march - ing in, I want to be in that
12
num - ber, when the saints go march - ing in.

Blue boogie

Moderato

Under a-rest

'Presto' means 'play as fast as you can'!

Presto

"HEY-PRESTO!"

HOT TIP

B down to A is one tone; B to B♭ is a semitone. Play these notes and listen to the difference.

Jingle bells

James Pierpont

Allegro

Jin-gle bells, jin-gle bells, jin-gle all the way. Oh, what fun it
is to ride a one-horse o-pen sleigh! Jin-gle bells, jin-gle bells,
jin-gle all the way. Oh, what fun it is to ride a one-horse o-pen sleigh!

STAGE 5

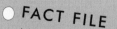

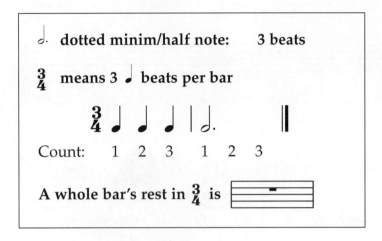

𝅗𝅥. dotted minim/half note:	3 beats
$\frac{3}{4}$ means 3 ♩ beats per bar	

Count: 1 2 3 1 2 3

A whole bar's rest in $\frac{3}{4}$ is 

FACT FILE

Most pieces of music are in a **key**.

The **key signature** is the group of sharps or flats shown at the beginning of every stave after the clef – it tells you what key the piece is in. **C major** doesn't have any sharps or flats in its key signature; **F major** has a key signature of one flat – B♭. All the Bs in a piece in F major will be flat, unless cancelled by a natural ♮.

𝄐 above a note means **pause** on that note for longer than its printed value.

Lento means **very slow.**

E 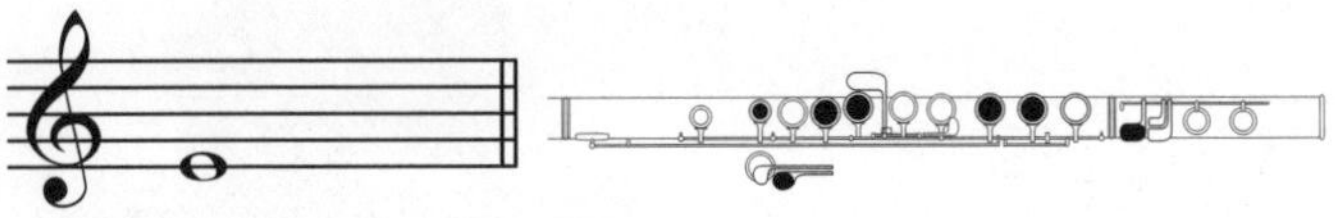

Your warm-up

Make up your own warm-up, using new note E, and write it on the stave below. Remember to choose a time signature.

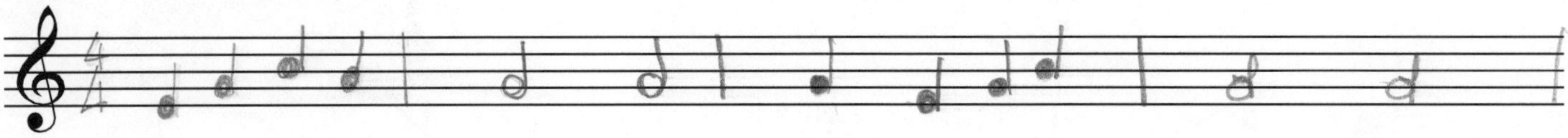

There's no escape

PIANO
ACCOMPANIMENT

TUNING
CHECK

QUALITY CONTROL CHECK

Listen carefully to each other to check your tuning.
Ask your teacher to help.

Funfair fanfare (trio)

Part 1
Part 2
Part 3

Wallie's waltz

Watch out for the key signature! All the Bs in this piece are flat unless otherwise indicated.

Moderato
4
12

Lotus flower

Lento
7
13

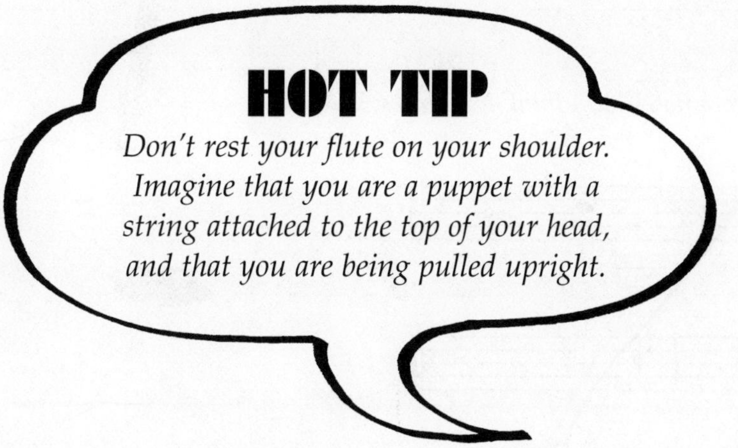
HOT TIP
Don't rest your flute on your shoulder. Imagine that you are a puppet with a string attached to the top of your head, and that you are being pulled upright.

¿QUIZ?

① Clap this rhythm:

② A 𝅗𝅥. is called a ____________________ and is worth 3 beats.

③ Write a piece in $\frac{3}{4}$ using the notes you know. Give it a title.

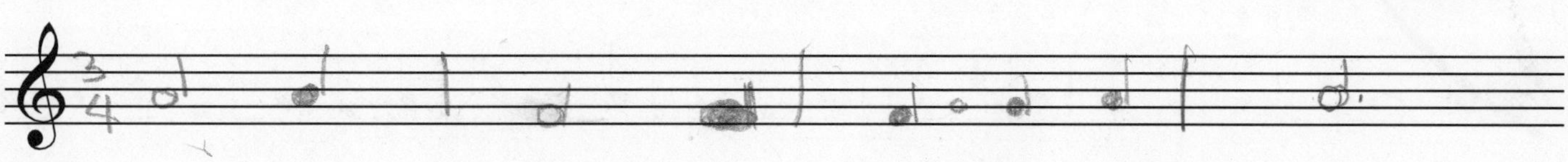

STAGE 6

FACT FILE

C means **common time**. It is another way of writing the $\frac{4}{4}$ time signature.

A dot under or over a note is called a **staccato** mark and means play the note short and bouncy. Say 'T—' instead of 'TUU—' to start the note.

𝄆 𝄇 These are **repeat signs** – the music in between them should be repeated.

Allegretto means **at a fairly quick speed.**

Pogo stick

Don't take a breath after every staccato note—still think in phrases.

TEACHER'S PART

Allegro
3

Figaro's tune

Wolfgang Amadeus Mozart

PIANO ACCOMPANIMENT

Allegretto
7
14

Play it again, Bob!

Allegro
6
11

Arabian nights

Lento
2
8
14

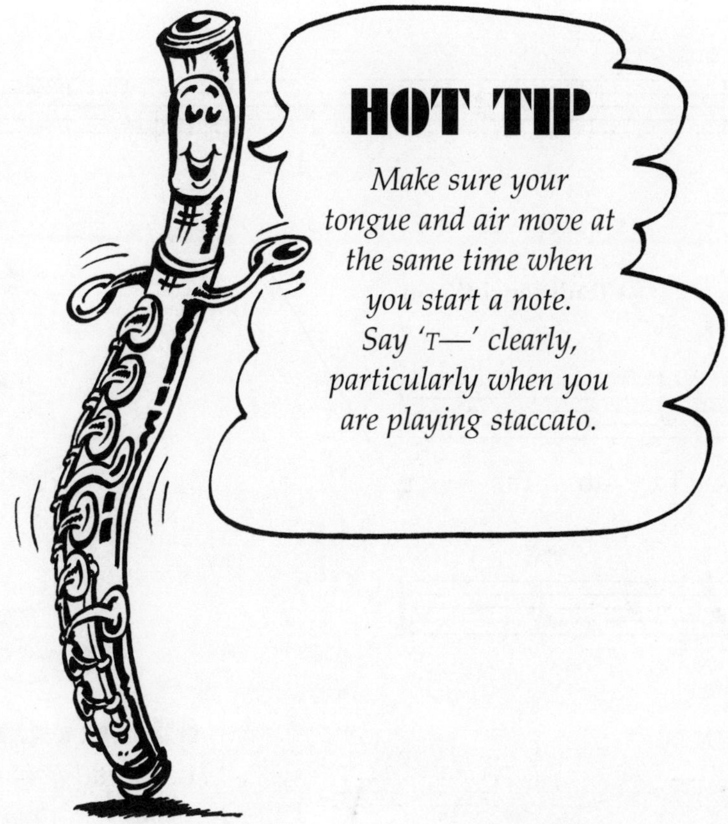
HOT TIP
Make sure your tongue and air move at the same time when you start a note. Say 'T—' clearly, particularly when you are playing staccato.

STAGE 7

FACT FILE

A **sharp sign** ♯ in front of a note raises it by a **semitone** ('half a tone'). F up to G is one tone; F to F♯ is a semitone. Listen to the difference.

A ⁀ **slur** sign over or under a group of notes means they should be played smoothly in one breath; only the first note is tongued. Say 'TA—AAH—'.

Andante means **at walking pace.**

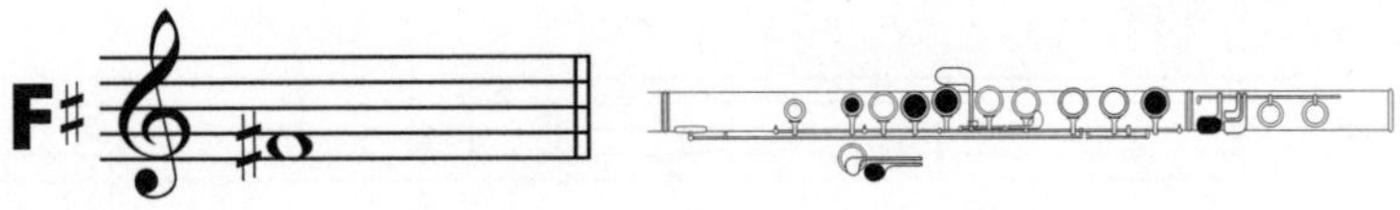
F♯

Warm-up 1

TEACHER'S PART

Warm-up 2

Make sure that your fingers move together when you play from E to F♯—keep your little finger still.

Spooks

PIANO ACCOMPANIMENT
Andante
9

Suo-gân

Traditional Welsh

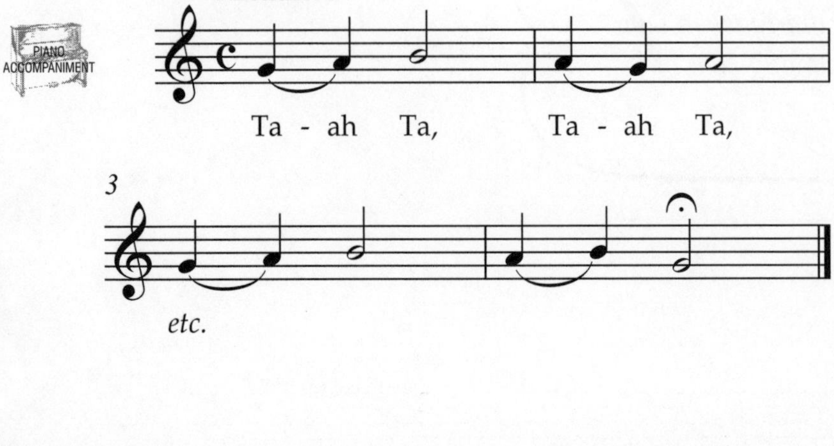
PIANO ACCOMPANIMENT
Andante
Ta - ah Ta, Ta - ah Ta,
3
etc.

TONE QUALITY CONTROL MANAGER

QUALITY CONTROL CHECK

The second note in the slur should be the same length and quality as the first.

PIANO
TUNA

A tuna day

Moderato

Strangers in the night

Bert Kaempfert

Moderato

© Copyright 1966 Champion Music Corporation & Screen Gems-Columbia Music Incorporated, USA. Universal/MCA Music Limited, 77 Fulham Palace Road, London W6 for the British Commonwealth (excluding Canada, Australasia and British territories in South America), South Africa, the Republic of Ireland and the Continent of Europe. (87.5%). Used by permission of Music Sales Ltd. All Rights Reserved. International Copyright Secured.

HOT TIP

Never clean your flute with silver polish—it can clog up the keys!

¿QUIZ?

① Give your teacher a lesson in how to play slurs.

② What does 'Presto' mean? ____________________

③ Make up your own piece using the notes you have learnt. Try to use staccatos and slurs.

STAGE 8

FACT FILE

G major has a key signature of one sharp – F♯. All the Fs in a piece in G major will be sharp, unless cancelled by a natural ♮.

Music doesn't always stay in the same time signature all the way through. Sometimes it might have different time signatures or be in **mixed meter**.

Low D

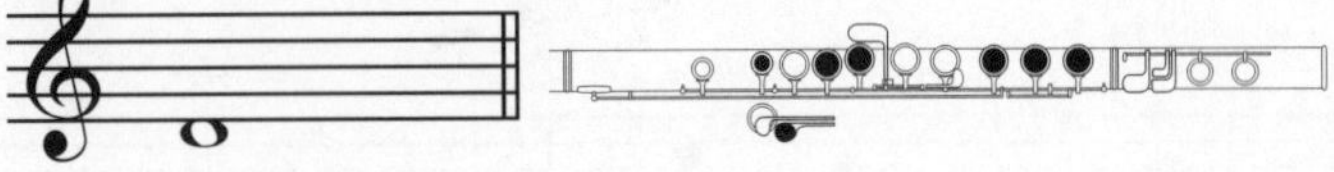

Finger fitness – Dodgy dealers

All the Fs in this piece are sharp. Make sure your little finger goes back on when you play from D to E.

This way and that

TEACHER'S PART

THIS WAY
THAT WAY

Big Ben

Can you complete this 'by ear'—with no music?

etc.

Crooked calypso

Allegro
8
15

The song of the Volga boatmen

Make sure that your fingers move exactly together as you play from F to low D.

Traditional Russian

Lento
2
6

Harem dance

Traditional

Allegro
3
7
10
13
17

STAGE 9

> **FACT FILE**
>
> A curved line joining two notes of the same pitch is called a **tie**. The duration of tied notes is their combined value.
>
> For example, hold ♩‿♩ for two beats.
>
> You now know the notes in a range of an **octave** (eight notes), from D to D.
>
> A **scale** (originally meaning 'ladder') is a set of notes that go up and down. A **pentatonic scale** has five different notes, and is used particularly in Eastern music.

Middle D

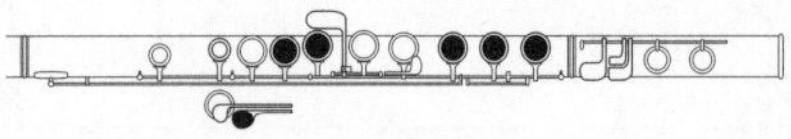

Pentatonic scale on D

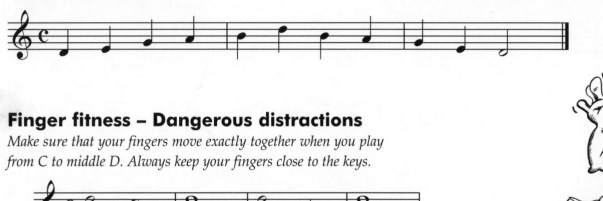

Finger fitness – Dangerous distractions

Make sure that your fingers move exactly together when you play from C to middle D. Always keep your fingers close to the keys.

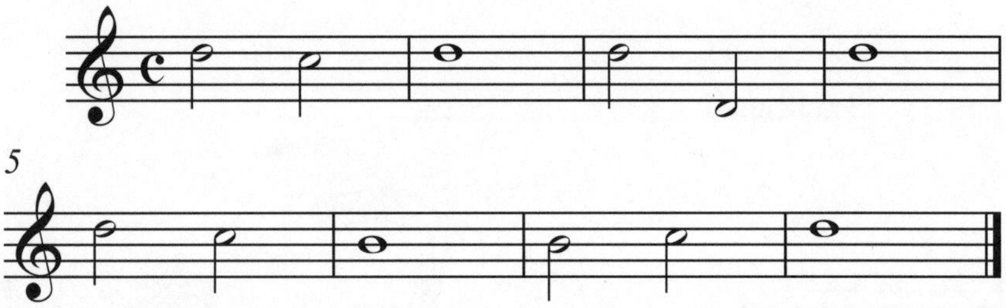

Seedy blues

Check that you have put the little finger back on again when you play from D to C.

PIANO ACCOMPANIMENT

Moderato

All tied up

Breathing is sometimes shown in music by the marking V. *Try adding your own in this piece.*

PIANO ACCOMPANIMENT

Allegro

DAISY, DAISY... YOU NAUGHTY DOG!!

Daisy Bell

Harry Dacre

Allegro

Chinese lanterns

¿QUIZ?

① Explain to your teacher the difference between a slur and a tie.

② Clap this rhythm: 

③ Write a piece using tied notes and either G major or F major key signature.
Finish the piece on the key note G or F (depending on the key).

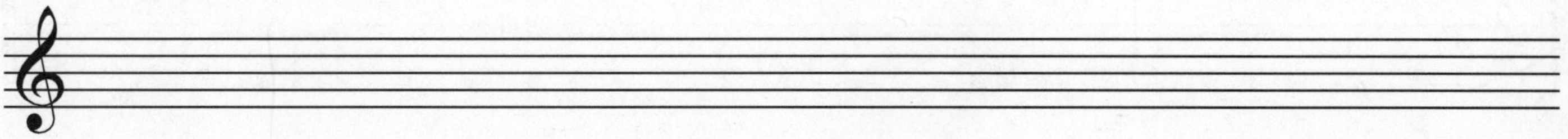

STAGE 10

FACT FILE

1st/2nd time bars. The first time through the piece, play the '1st time' bars, then repeat; the second time through, leave out the '1st time' bars and go straight to the '2nd time' bars.

D.S. or ***D.𝄋*** stands for ***dal segno*** and means 'from the sign'. ***D.S. al Fine*** means 'go back to the 𝄋 sign and play until you see the ***Fine*** sign, where you should end the piece'.

f (***forte***) means **loud**. ***p*** (***piano***) means **quiet**. These volume instructions are called **dynamics**.

G♯

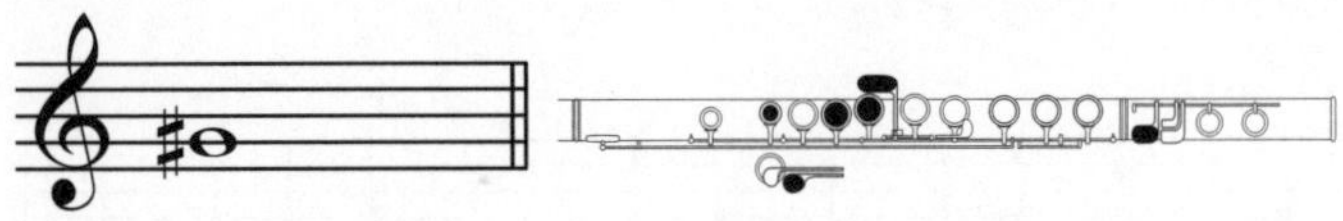

 **quaver/eighth note:** **½ beat**

Clap: 

Count: 1 & 2 & 3 & 4 & 1 & 2 & 3 & 4 &

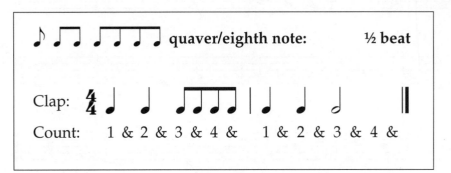

QUALITY CONTROL CHECK

Remember that a group of tongued notes is really just a long note, broken up. Your sound quality should remain the same throughout.

SOUND LEVELS

I like bread and butter

PIANO ACCOMPANIMENT

Moorish dance (duet)

Make sure you take the G♯ key off when you have finished playing G♯.

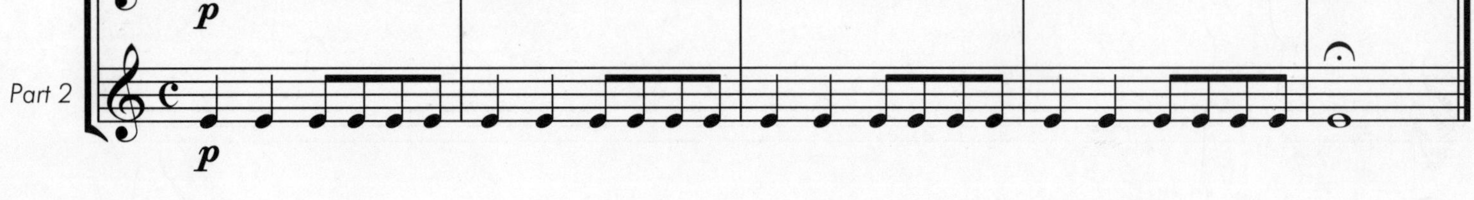
Part 1
Part 2

Blue riff

f (2nd time p)
3
1.
2.

DUN-ROAMIN'
Gnome & Away

The roamin' gnomes

Maybe they're looking for Apple Pies and Custard …

Moderato
4
f
8
12
p
17
f

Clown dance

With humour
2
f
p
6
Fine
f
p
f
11
D. 𝄋 al Fine
f
p
f

STAGE 11

> **FACT FILE**
>
> **D major** has a key signature of two sharps – F♯ and C♯ – just think of **F**ish and **C**hips! The scale of D major includes all the notes in the **key** of D major. An **arpeggio** is made up of the first, third and fifth note of the scale.
>
> means play the note with force. The > sign is called an **accent**.
>
> Not all music starts on the first beat of the bar. Notes that come before the first full bar are called **upbeats**; the value of the upbeat is taken away from the last bar of the piece.

Middle C♯

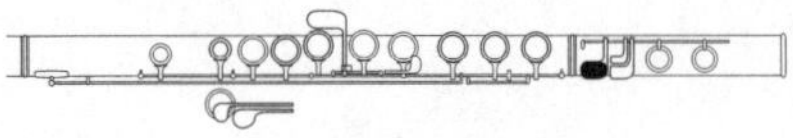

Clap: 

Count: 1 & 2 & 3 & 1 & 2 & 3 & 1 & 2 & 3 &

Warm-up

Keep your flute steady by supporting it with your left-hand first finger and the little finger of your right hand.

TEACHER'S PART

I C sharps ahead (duet)

Part 1
Part 2

D major scale and arpeggio

It's jolly to swing (round for 3 players)

A round is a piece in which several players have the same music but start one after the other. In this piece, start four bars apart.

1.
2.
6
3.

The first Nowell

Traditional English

f
6
p
11
f

LONDON
6½ MILES
LONDON
6½ MILES

Turn again, Whittington (round for 3 players)

Traditional English

1.
2.
3.

¿QUIZ?

① Can you say all the notes of the D major scale and then play it by memory? Do the same with the arpeggio.

② How many different ways can you play the scale—staccato, slurred or upside down (starting with the top note)?

③ Clap a rhythm: 

HOT TIP

Make sure that you tongue lightly and clearly when you are playing quavers/eighth notes.

CONCERT PIECES

Awake, my love

German folksong arranged by Johannes Brahms

Flowing

PIANO ACCOMPANIMENT
p
4
8
f
12
p
2

Strawberries and cream

Paul Harris

Allegro

PIANO ACCOMPANIMENT
f
p
6
f
10
14
p
18
f

A road to somewhere

Peter Cowdrey

Moderato

Free as a bird

Pam Wedgwood

Jazz waltz

STAGE 12

> **FACT FILE**
>
> ***D.C.*** stands for ***da capo*** and means 'go back to the beginning'.
>
> ***Rit.*** stands for ***ritardando*** and means 'slow down'. ***A tempo*** means 'back to the original speed'.
>
> A slur with staccato dots indicates legato tonguing: move your tongue with a slower movement and say 'DHOAH—' to start the note (it should sound like a bell tolling).
>
> ***Legato*** means 'play smoothly with no break between the notes'.
>
> A **comma** ❜ above the stave means have a short break or breath.

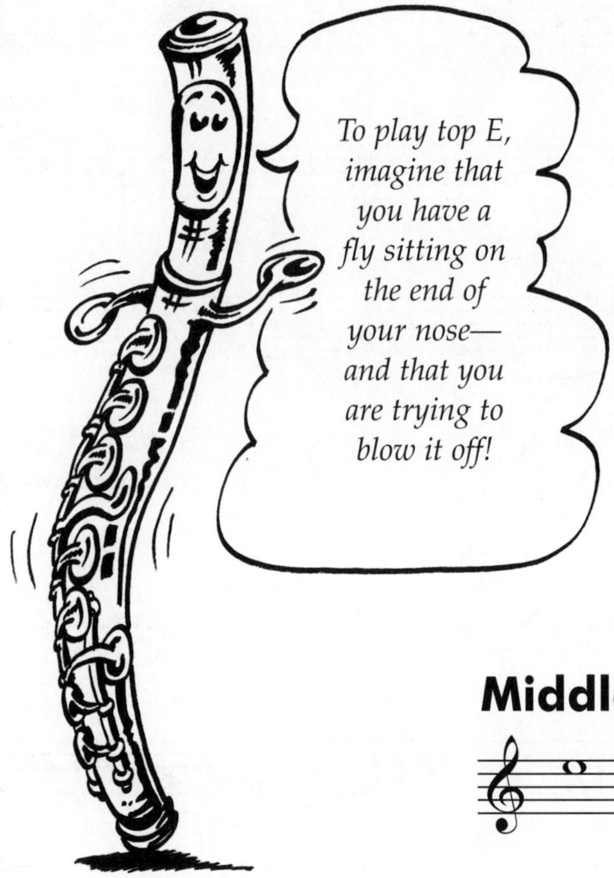
To play top E, imagine that you have a fly sitting on the end of your nose—and that you are trying to blow it off!

Middle E

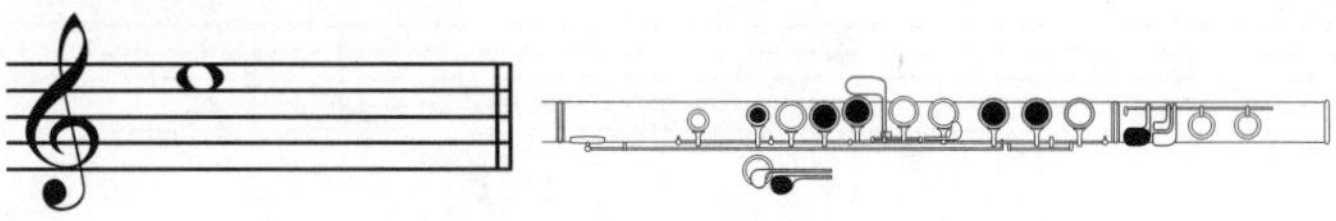

Warm-up (duet)

Part 1
Part 2

Easy does it

PIANO ACCOMPANIMENT
Andante
p
5
rit.

Shortnin' bread

Allegro
f
5

Quem pastores (duet)

Traditional French

Experiment with this piece, using staccato and then legato tonguing. Decide which suits the mood of the piece best.

Moderato
Part 1
Part 2
p
p
8

From Neasden with love

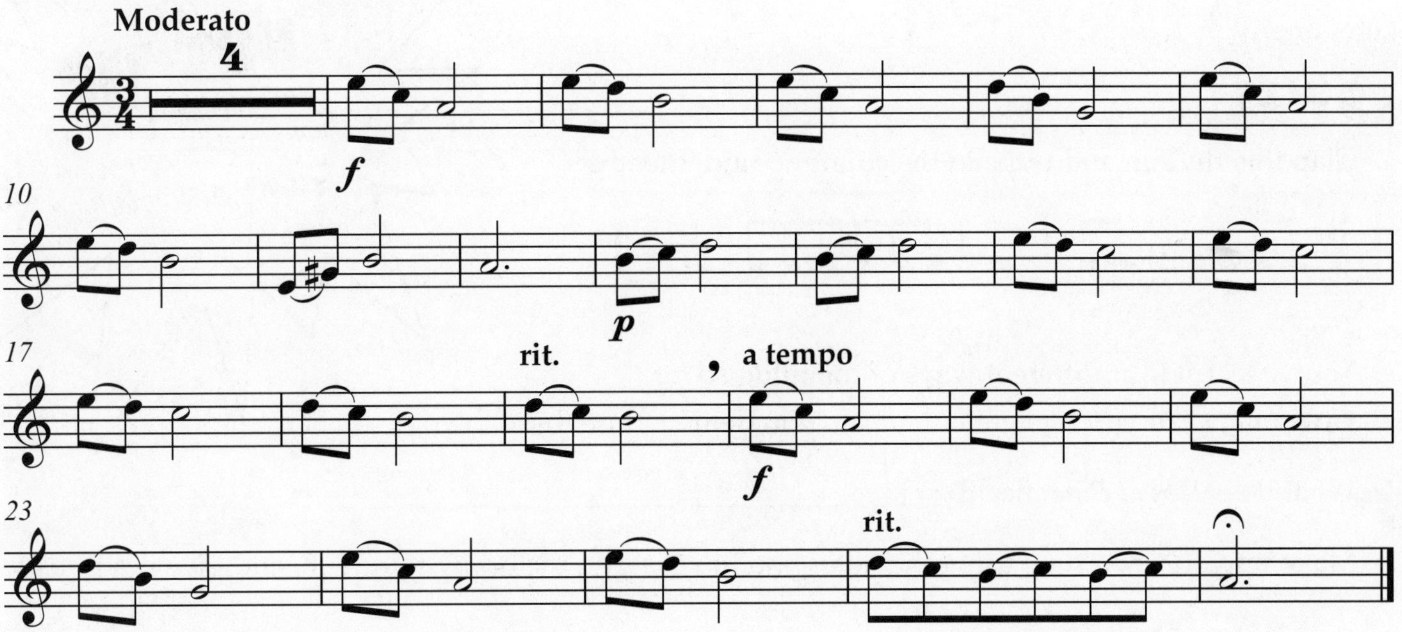
Moderato
4
f
10
p
17
rit.
a tempo
f
23
rit.

PRACTISING FLEXIBLE FRIENDS

cresc.
sf
f
p
mf
dim.
mp

Play them using different dynamics and articulations each time—

staccato

legato tonguing

accents

piano

forte

Flexible friends – flute gymnastics

5

HOT TIP

Always make sure that your little finger is on when you play middle E.

¿QUIZ?

① Clap this rhythm and write in the counting underneath:

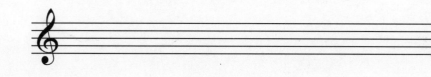

② You've learnt four different ways of tonguing so far.
How many can you remember and can you demonstrate these to your teacher?

③ What does ***D.𝄋 al Fine*** mean? ______________________________

④ Make up your own tune using the notes you have learnt, including middle E, and give it a title.

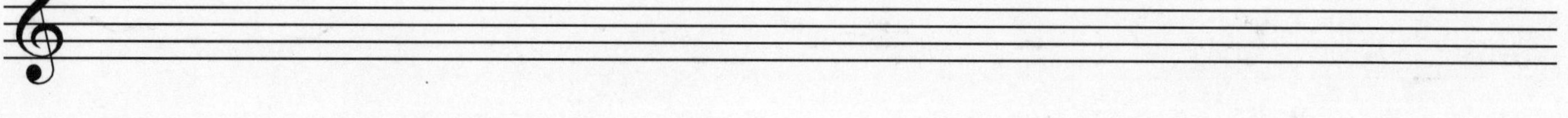

STAGE 13

FACT FILE

mp (*mezzopiano*) means **quite soft.**

mf (*mezzoforte*) means **quite loud.**

Middle F

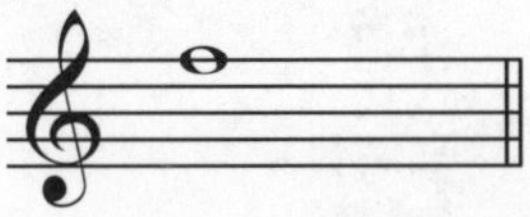

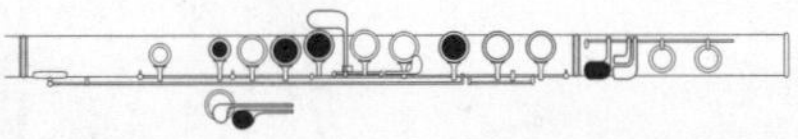

𝄾 **quaver/eighth note rest:** **½ beat**

Clap:

Count: 1 & 2 & 3 & 4 & 1 & 2 & 3 & 4 &

QUALITY
CONTROL
CHECK
Listen carefully to the quality of your high notes: if you move your lower lip too much, the sound will become thin and airy.

Warm-up

Feelin' funky – F major scale

TEACHER'S PART

Feelin' fine – F major arpeggio

TEACHER'S PART

Great 'F'ort required

PIANO
MPANIMENT

QUIET
PLEASE

Quelle est cette odeur agréable?

Traditional French

Andante
PIANO ACCOMPANIMENT
mp
6
Fine
mf
12
D.C. al Fine

Rest assured

Moderato
PIANO ACCOMPANIMENT
mp
5
mf
f

The Can-Can from *Orpheus in the Underworld*

Jacques Offenbach

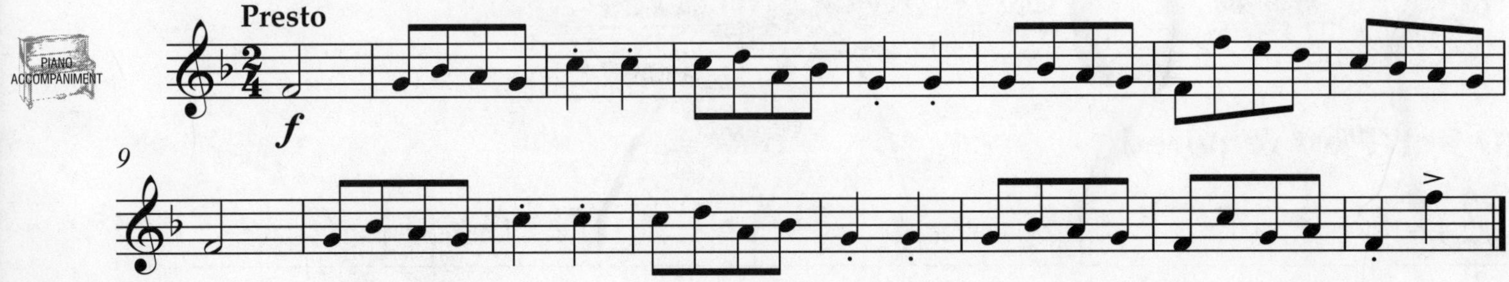
Presto
PIANO ACCOMPANIMENT
f
9

Jazzmin's waltz

PIANO ACCOMPANIMENT
mp
9
mf
17
mp

Flexible friends – flute gymnastics

3
5
7

HOT TIP

Avoid eating sweets before—or during—your flute practice. Remember, your teeth are important!

TONE

PRACTICE

Practise a little every day rather than one really long practice every few days.

Practise the difficult bits as well as the easier bits.

Play the difficult bits slowly until they become easy.

Always play something just for fun.

Learn your pieces from memory.

Make your own practice chart, so you can tick the items off as you practise them each day.

STAGE 14

> **FACT FILE**
>
> *Crescendo* (*cresc.*) means gradually getting louder.
>
> *Diminuendo* (*dim.*) means gradually getting quieter.

Middle F♯

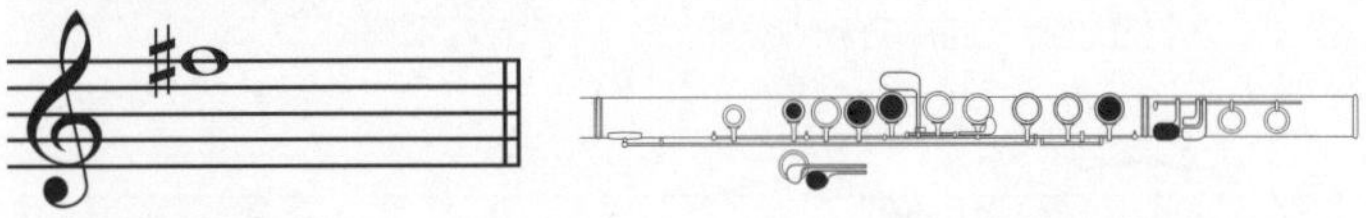

Middle G

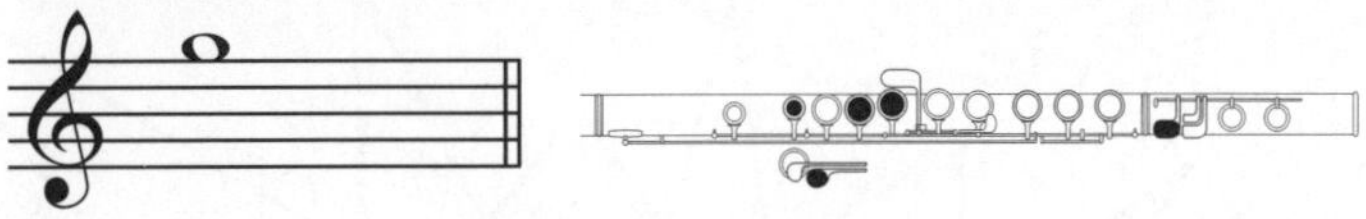

Warm-up (duet)

Part 1
Part 2

Gorgeous George

PIANO ACCOMPANIMENT
2
mf

Groovin' grannies – G major scale

TEACHER'S PART

Gymnastic gerbils – G major arpeggio

TEACHER'S PART

SPRING MUST BE IN THE AIR...
YES, I JUST CAUGHT SIGHT OF SOME EARLY BLOOMERS!

Slane

Traditional Irish

Moderato

Minuet from *Alcina*

George Frideric Handel

Moderato

Only the heart aches (duet)

Traditional American

Allegro
Part 1
Part 2

Wistful waltz

Allegro moderato

PIANO ACCOMPANIMENT
5

Flexible friends – flute gymnastics

5

STOPWATCH CHALLENGE

What's the quietest,
longest note you can play?

What's the **loudest**,
longest note you can play?

Tear a 3cm-wide strip of newspaper about 30cm long and hold it 15cm away from your nose. Gently blow against the strip of paper: how long you can hold the paper steady at 45°?

Time each other using a stopwatch!

HOT TIP

Can you play any of the pieces you have learnt so far from memory? It's always good to have a party piece up your sleeve!

¿QUIZ?

① Can you play the scales of F major and G major without looking at the music?

② Clap the following rhythm: 

③ What do the following tempo markings mean?

Allegretto ________________ ***Moderato*** ________________

Andante ________________ ***Presto*** ________________

STAGE 15

FACT FILE

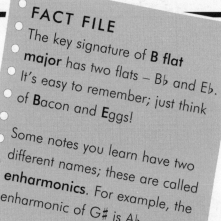

The key signature of **B flat major** has two flats – B♭ and E♭. It's easy to remember; just think of **B**acon and **E**ggs!

Some notes you learn have two different names; these are called **enharmonics**. For example, the enharmonic of G♯ is A♭.

Low E♭ 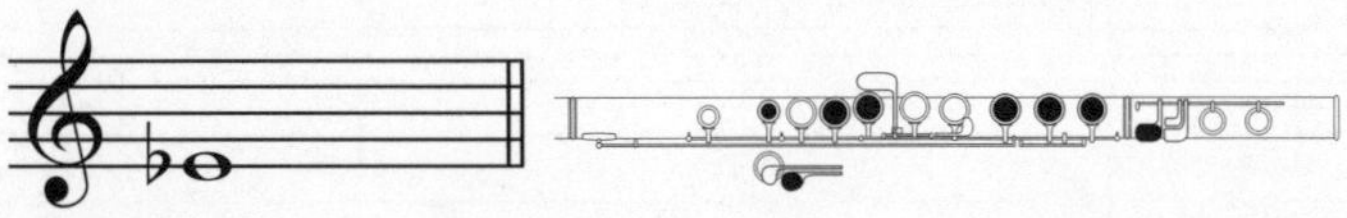

Middle E♭ 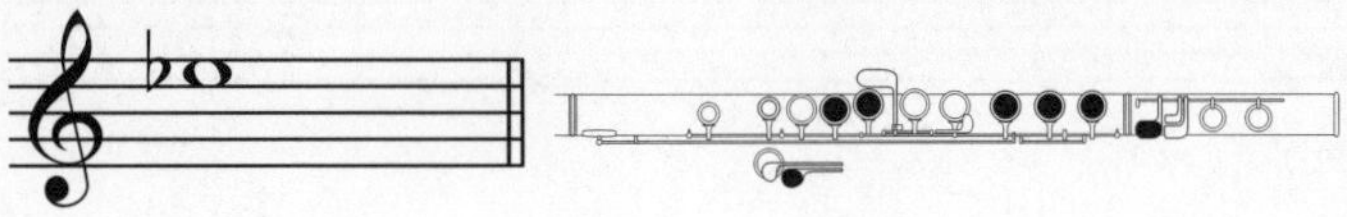

A dot after a note makes its duration half as long again, so: 

Clap: 

Count: 1 & 2 & 3 & 4 & 1 & 2 & 3 & 4 &

Warm-up

ACHER'S PART

The earwig étude

PIANO MPANIMENT

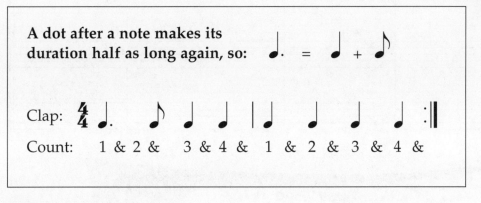

LESSON 1
FIRST MAKE CERTAIN YOU ARE PLAYING A FLUTE!

Spooky moment

Allegro misterioso

PIANO MPANIMENT

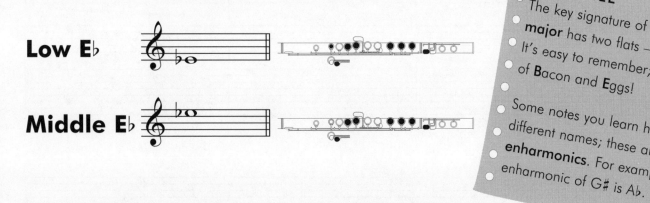

Entrance of the eloquent elephants (trio)

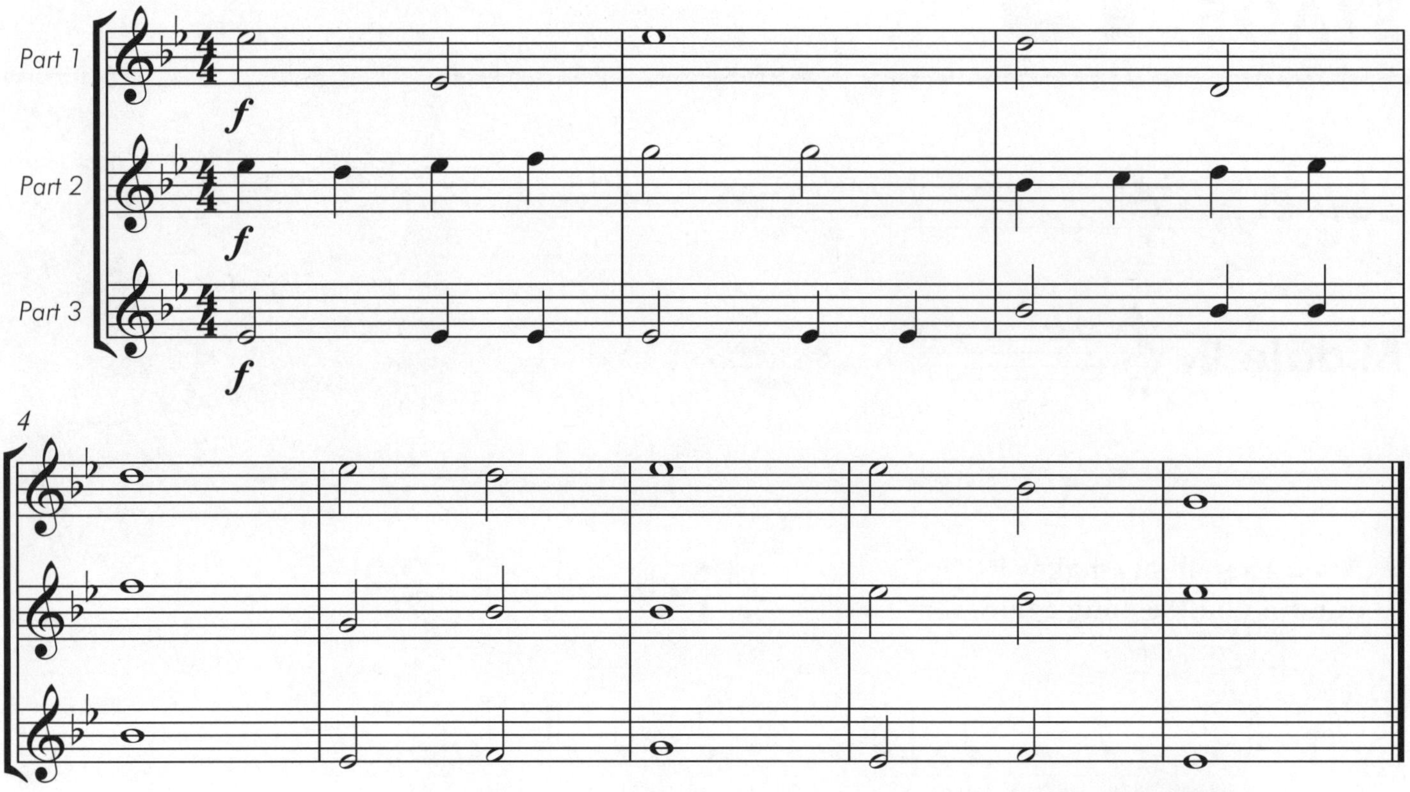
Part 1
Part 2
Part 3
f
f
f
4

OI... JUST FOR ONCE, WHY DON'T YOU SING 'OVER THE HILLS AND FAR AWAY'!
WWOAW

All through the night

Traditional Welsh

PIANO ACCOMPANIMENT

Andante
mf
mf
7
Fine
mp
D. 𝄋 al Fine

You-rang-a-tango

Nigel Morley

Flexible friends – flute gymnastics

HOT TIP

Always make sure that you are using the correct fingering for middle E♭. The left-hand first finger must be up for middle E♭.

STAGE 16

FACT FILE

For every major scale there is a **minor** scale that shares the same key signature. The major scale sounds happy and the minor scale sounds sad. The minor scale in Stage 16 is E minor (harmonic and melodic), and has the same key signature – F♯ – as G major. E minor is therefore known as the **relative minor** of G major.

D♯ is the **enharmonic** of E♭.

Poco moto means **a little motion** or **keep moving.**

Low D♯

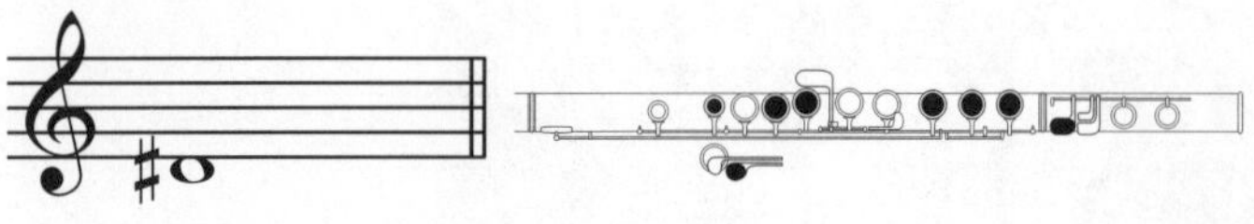

Middle D♯

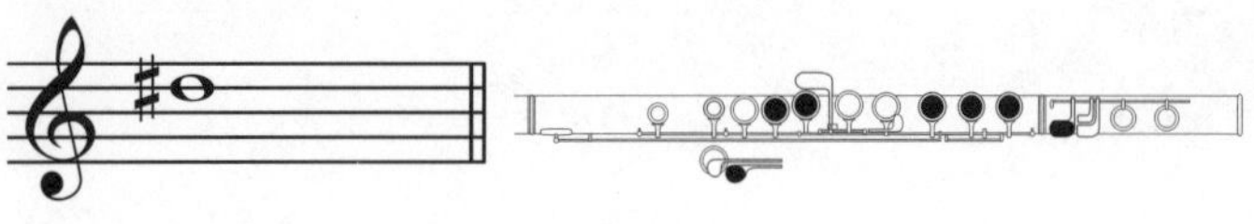

Warm-up (duet)

1.
2.
Part 1
Part 2

The energetic eccentric – E minor scale (harmonic)

Don't take your little finger off when you play E minor scale and arpeggio.

TEACHER'S PART

The elegant elephant – E minor scale (melodic)

TEACHER'S PART

The envious envelope – E minor arpeggio

TEACHER'S PART

ALL I GET IS A STAMP ON MY HEAD!

Scarborough fair

Traditional English

Moderato
4
mp
10
mf
17
dim.
p

King Tut's tap-dancing team

Allegro
2
f
6
10
Fine
mf
15
D. 𝄋 al Fine
p

Für Elise

Ludwig van Beethoven

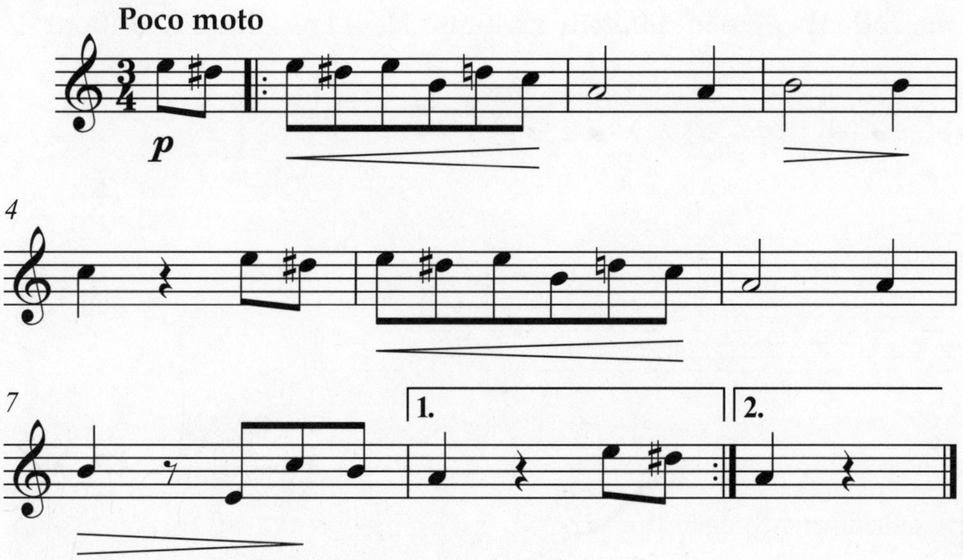
Poco moto
p
4
7
1.
2.

Listen carefully when you play from middle E to middle D♯; are the notes even in sound and quality?

Flexible friends – flute gymnastics

Remember to practise using different dynamics and articulations each time.

Moderato
3
6

cresc.
sf
f
p
mf
dim.
mp

LONG NOTES

Play long notes at the start of every practice; they will help you learn to control the sound you make on the flute. Start them quietly and then make them as loud as possible before ending quietly.

Make each note as long and as beautiful as you can.

¿QUIZ?

① Can you play your E minor scale and arpeggio in different rhythms? Here are some suggestions:

or
or

② Play the following notes:

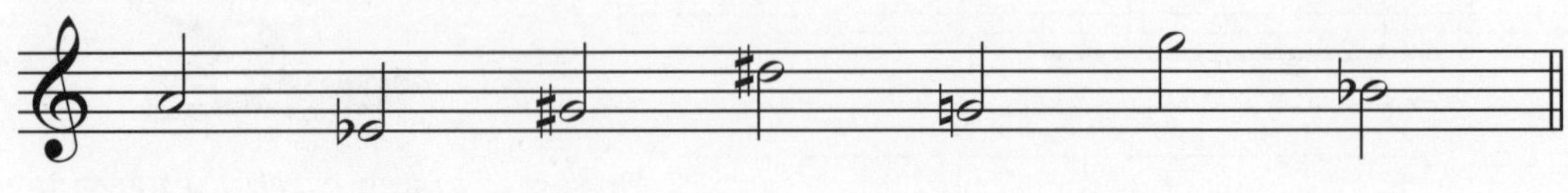

③ Now write down the note names underneath each one.

STAGE 17

FACT FILE

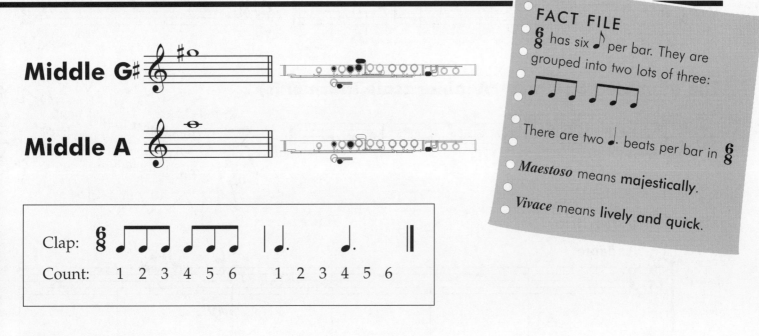

- 6/8 has six ♪ per bar. They are grouped into two lots of three:

- There are two ♩. beats per bar in 6/8
- *Maestoso* means **majestically.**
- *Vivace* means **lively and quick.**

Middle G♯

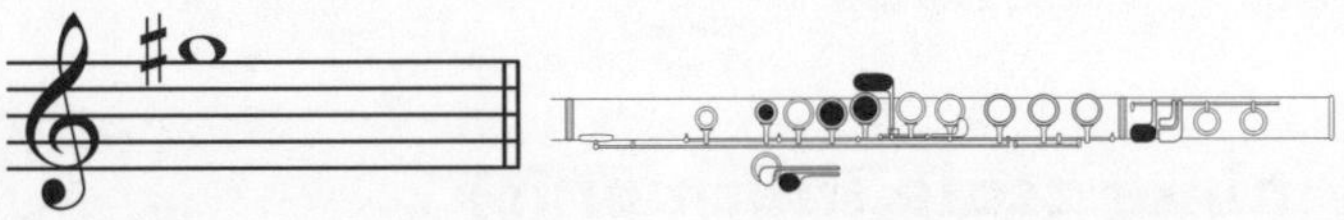

Middle A

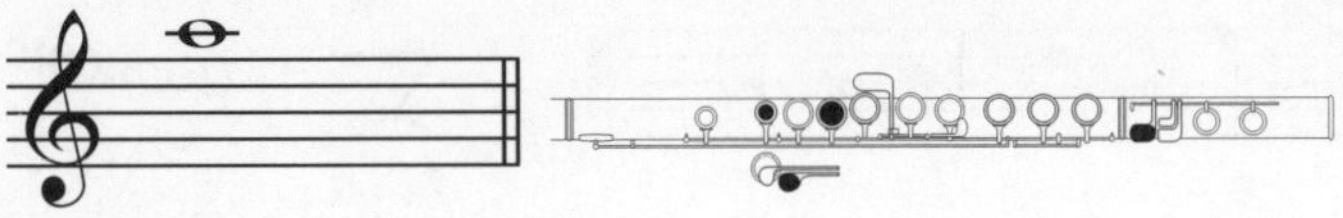

Clap:

Count: 1 2 3 4 5 6 1 2 3 4 5 6

Warm-up (duet)

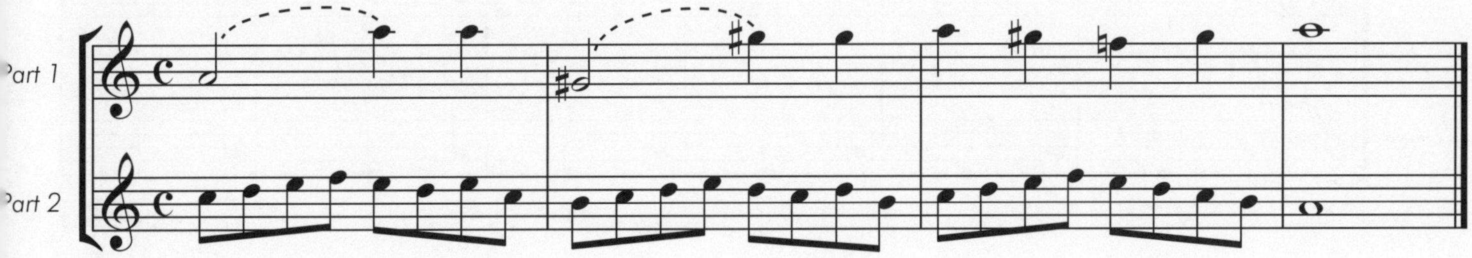
Part 1
Part 2

Spam and sausage fanfare

Maestoso
rit.
Sau - sa - ges, sau - sa - ges, sau - sa - ges, spam.

BLOTTO
LAGER
EASY-
SQUEEZE
TOMATO
KETCHUP

The adventurous acrobat – A minor scale (melodic)

TEACHER'S PART

The angelic apricot – A minor arpeggio

The animated apeman – A minor scale (harmonic)

TEACHER'S PART

Remember to take your G♯ key off when you have finished playing the note.

Siberian song (trio)

Andante
Part 1
Part 2
Part 3
mp
p
p
7
14

Rondo *from* Horn Concerto No.4

Wolfgang Amadeus Mozart

Allegro vivace
p
5

Moment triste

Lento
2
p
7

Flexible friends – flute gymnastics

5

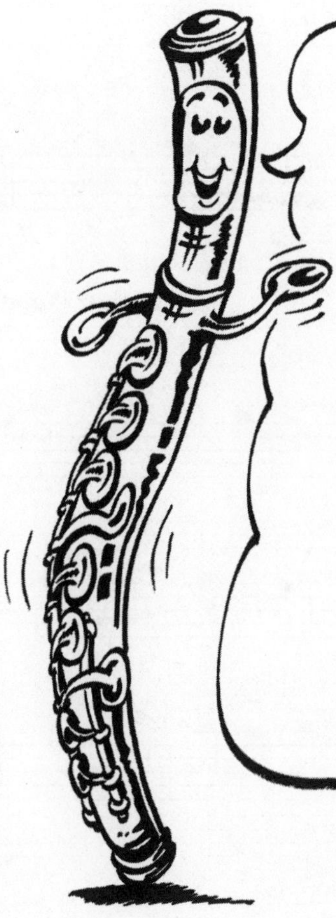

SCALES AND ARPEGGIOS …

… will give you the 'building bricks' of music—learn all your scales and arpeggios really well, and eventually you will be able to play most of the flute music that has ever been written.

- Use scales to improve your sound, tonguing and dynamics.
- Find lots of different ways to play your scales—tongued, slurred, upside down (no, not standing on your head!), in different rhythms …
- Work through Paul Harris's *Improve your scales!* for flute for some great ideas.
- And finally, learn your scales from memory!

STAGE 18

FACT FILE

Giocoso means **playful and humorous.**

The **Gymnopédies** were a set of piano pieces written by Erik Satie (1866–1925). The *gymnopaidiai* was a festival at ancient Sparta.

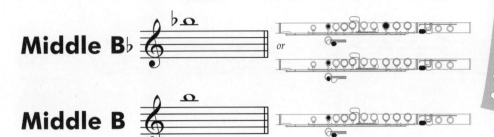

Middle B♭

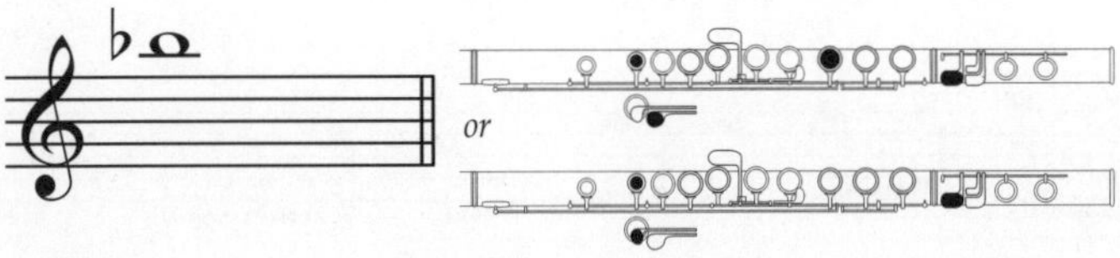
or

Middle B

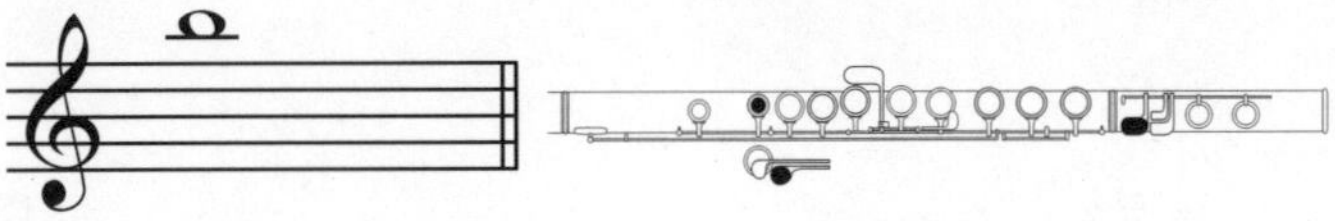

High C

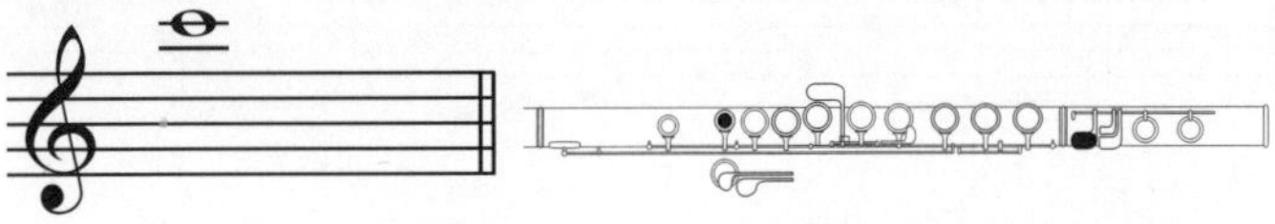

SOUND LEVELS

QUALITY CONTROL CHECK

Listen carefully to your top notes; try not to overblow. Always aim to make a beautiful sound!

Warm-up (duet)

Part 1
Part 2

Rumpty tumpty

Allegro

PIANO ACCOMPANIMENT

Theme from *The Archers*

Arthur Wood

Allegro giocoso

PIANO ACCOMPANIMENT
f
6
mf
11
f

© Copyright 1925 by Boosey & Co. Ltd. Reproduced by permission of Boosey & Hawkes Music Publishers Ltd.

Gymnopédie

Moderato
4
mp
9
15

(I CAN'T GET NO SATIESFACTION !)

When Alan met Sally

Sally Adams & Alan Gout

Moderato
2
p
9
15
mf
21
p
25

Flexible friends (The galloping galways) – flute gymnastics

Allegro
5
9
13

Know your tunes

Fill in the name and the key of each tune—and then finish each one by memory!

Tune 1: ______________________ Key: __________

Tune 2: ______________________ Key: __________

¿QUIZ?

① A ♩. in 6/8 is worth ____beats when you are counting in ♪

② Clap the following rhythm and write the counting underneath:

Count:

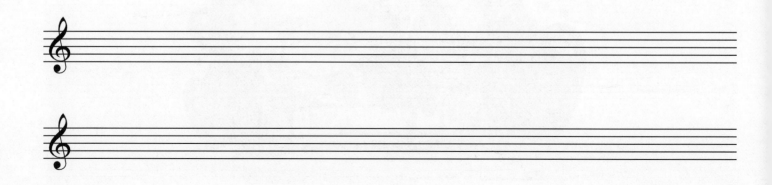

③ Can you write a piece in 6/8 using the rhythms you know? Remember to give it some dynamics and articulation—and a title.

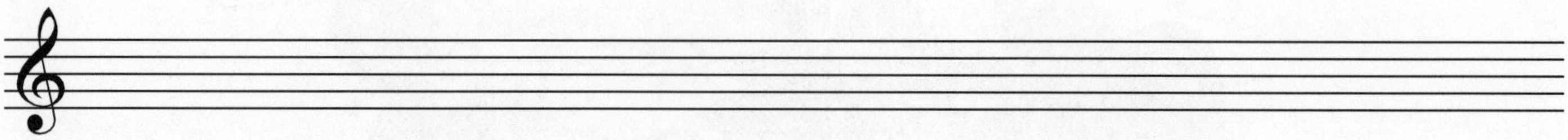

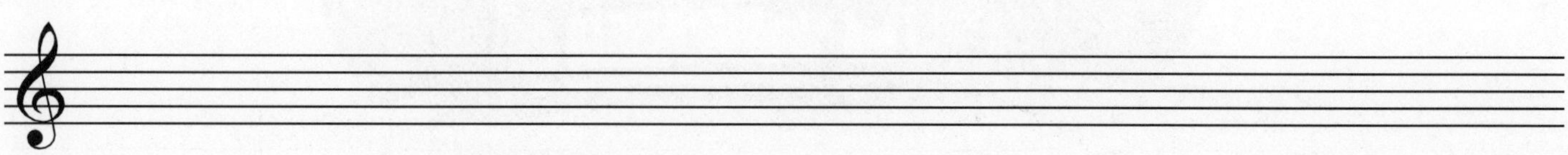

STAGE 19

FACT FILE

Swing is a vital ingredient of jazz. When you play swing ♪ make the first ♪ twice as long as the second (sometimes shown by ♫ = ♩♪ (triplet)). To get the feel of swing listen to some jazz – think of the cool flute solo in *The Pink Panther*.

An **off beat** is a note that goes against the beat. Another name for this is a **syncopated note**.

Subtle syncopation

3

NOW THEN, BOYS... PLAYTIME'S OVER, TIME TO GET BACK TO WORK... UM, PLEASE... BOYS...
Saint Nitwits School of VERY SERIOUS MUSIC
STAFF CAR PARK

Playtime rag

Alan Gout

Allegro
mf (f on D.C.)
6
11
15
Fine
19
23
28
D.C. al Fine

Blues scale on A

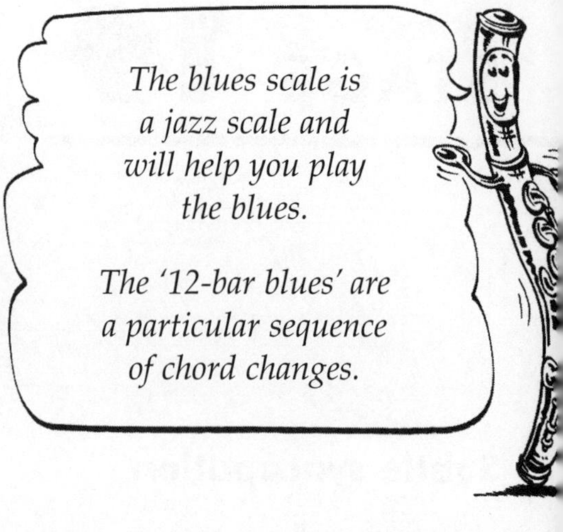
The blues scale is
a jazz scale and
will help you play
the blues.
The '12-bar blues' are
a particular sequence
of chord changes.

Blues scale on E

A♯ is the enharmonic of B♭. Try using the long fingering for this note.

Swing it 1

Swing it 2

Emily's half-term blues

Have a go at making up, or 'improvising', your own 12-bar blues the 2nd time round.
Start with just a couple of notes from the note bank and one of the rhythms.

PIANO ACCOMPANIMENT
Funky
2
E
mf
E
E
6
E
A
A
E
E
11
B
A
E
D. 𝄋 for
improvisation
Ending

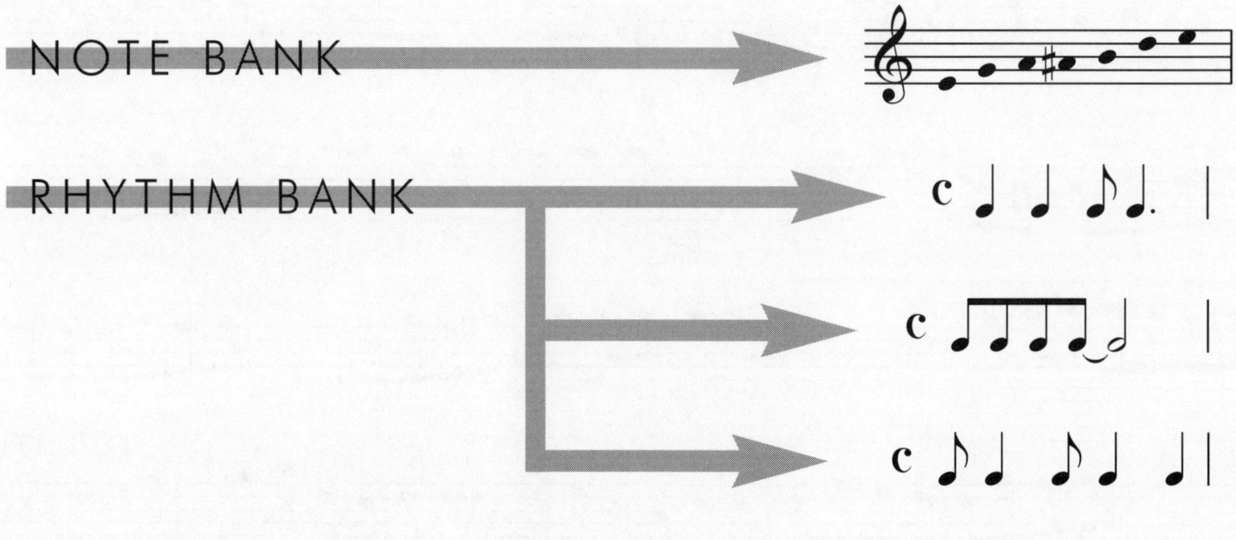
NOTE BANK
RHYTHM BANK

Sidewalk swing (duet)

Sarah Watts

swung quavers
Part 1
Part 2

STAGE 20

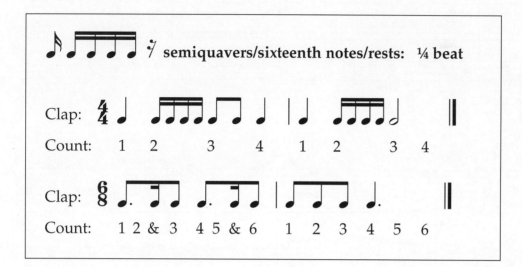

 semiquavers/sixteenth notes/rests: ¼ beat

Clap: 

Count: 1 2 3 4 1 2 3 4

Clap: 

Count: 1 2 & 3 4 5 & 6 1 2 3 4 5 6

FACT FILE

A horizontal line above or below a note is called a **tenuto** mark and means 'lean on the note'.

High C♯ 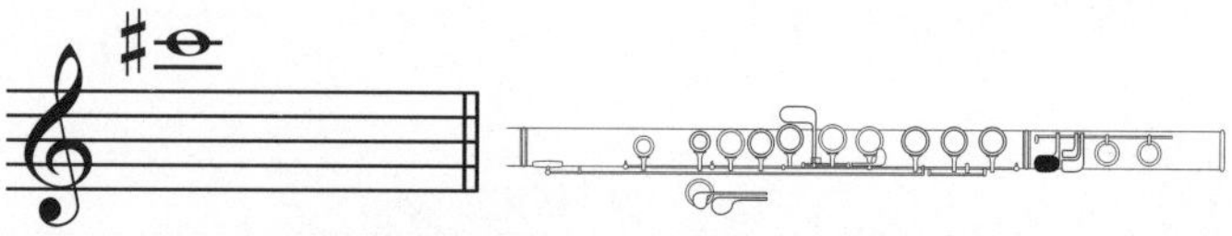

High D 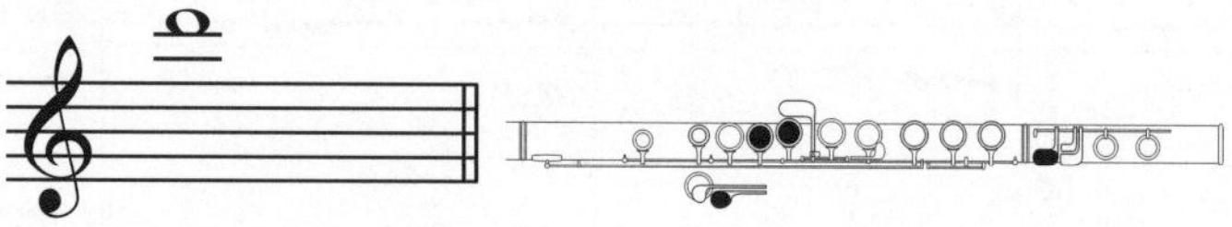

TONE
QUALITY CONTROL MANAGER

QUALITY CONTROL CHECK

Listen carefully to the quality of your top C♯; you need a faster air speed to play top C♯ than D.

Warm-up (duet)

Part 1
Part 2

D major scale – 2 octaves

D major arpeggio – 2 octaves

The battle cry of the aphids (trio)

Part 1
ff Slug, Ca - ter - pil - lar, Green - fly, Slug
etc.
Part 2
ff
Part 3
ff
3

HOW DO YOU LIKE THESE TWO LIPS?
VERY NICE, MY DEAR... BUT THEY'RE ROSES!

Embouchures from Amsterdam (duet)

Do you know what your embouchure is? If not, ask your teacher!

art 1
mp
mf
art 2
mp
mf

Greensleeves

attributed to **Henry VIII**

PIANO ACCOMPANIMENT
Moderato
p
7
mf
13
rit.

Theme from *Blackadder*

Howard Goodall

PIANO ACCOMPANIMENT
Moderato
mf
5
mf
9
p
f
14

© Copyright 1983 Noel Gay Music Company Limited, 8/9 Frith Street, London W1.
Used by permission of Music Sales Ltd. All Rights Reserved. International Copyright Secured.

Flexible friends – flute gymnastics

5

FOOTNOTES ...

Low C♯

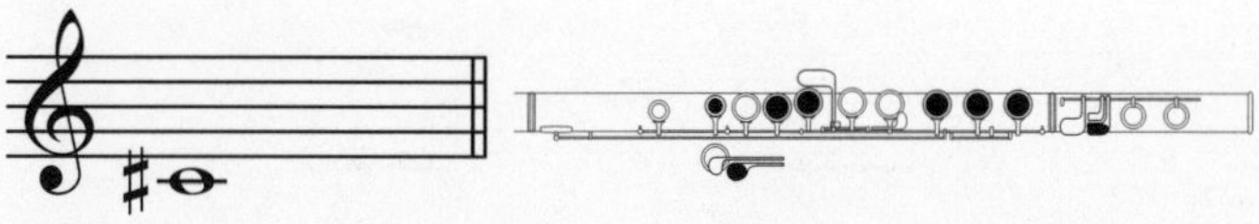

Low C

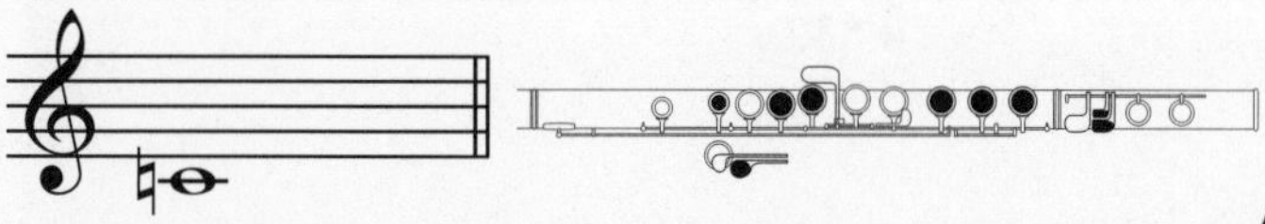

TONE
TUNING CHECK.

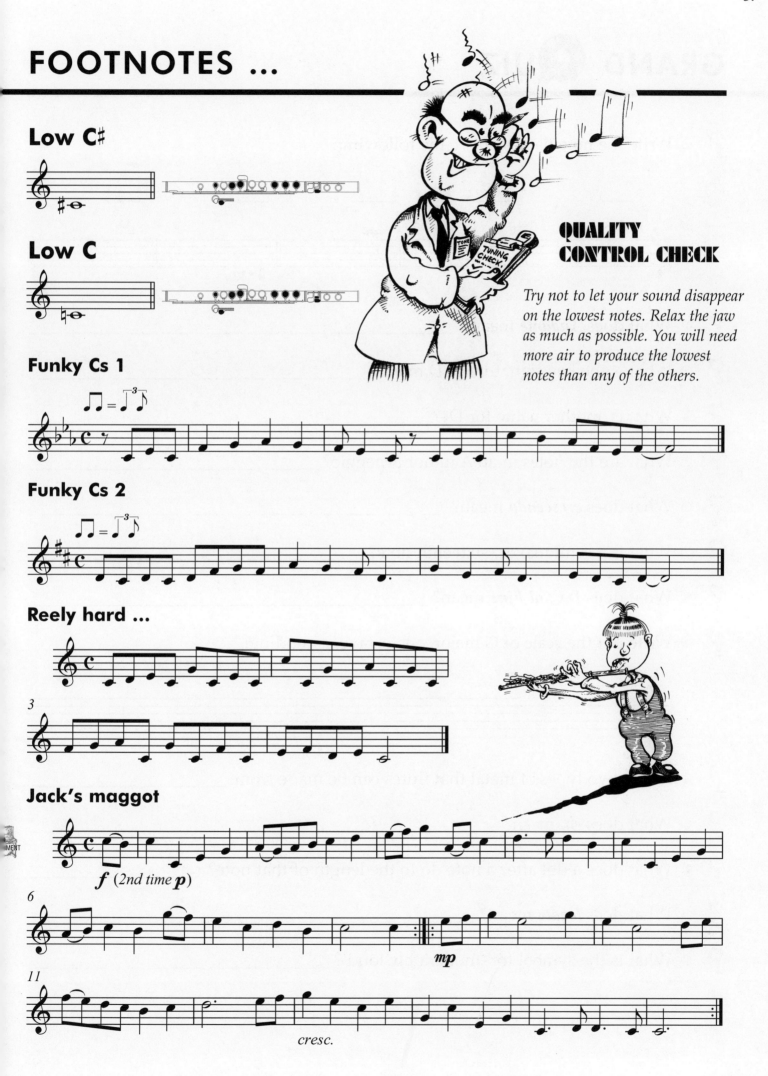

QUALITY CONTROL CHECK

Try not to let your sound disappear on the lowest notes. Relax the jaw as much as possible. You will need more air to produce the lowest notes than any of the others.

Funky Cs 1

Funky Cs 2

Reely hard ...

Jack's maggot

f (2nd time p)
6
mp
11
cresc.

GRAND QUIZ

① Write the note names above the following:

② What does ***Andante*** mean? ______

③ What is the key signature of D major? ______

④ What is another name for D♯? ______

⑤ What are the notes in an A minor arpeggio? ______

⑥ What does ***crescendo*** mean? ______

⑦ What is a semiquaver/sixteenth note? ______

⑧ What does ***D.C. al Fine*** mean? ______

⑨ Write out the scale of G major, one octave, ascending:

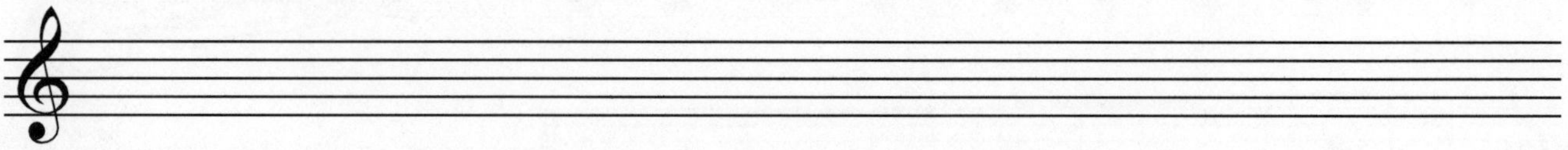

⑩ Name two types of metal that flutes can be made from: ______

⑪ What does ***rit.*** mean? ______

⑫ What does a dot after a note do to the length of that note? ______

⑬ What does ***legato*** mean? ______

⑭ What is the symbol for 'moderately loud'? ______

CONCERT PIECES

Spanish lullaby

Peter Cowdrey

Moderato
mf
5
p
9
f
p
15
rit.
dim.

Menuett

Anonymous

mf
7
p
cresc.
13
mf
p
19
cresc.
25
mf
31
f

No.3 from *Four Irish Dances*

Malcolm Arnold

Piacevole (pleasantly)

PIANO ACCOMPANIMENT
p
f
dim.
7
p
f
mp
14
mp
mp
f
20
p
25
f dim.
30
f
p
37
f
43
p
rall.

© 1986 by Faber Music Ltd.
This arrangement © 2002 by Faber Music Ltd.

La forêt argentée

Sally Adams

Misterioso
4
mf
9
p
mf
14
18
rit.
a tempo
p
24
28
mf
34
ad lib.

FINGERING CHART

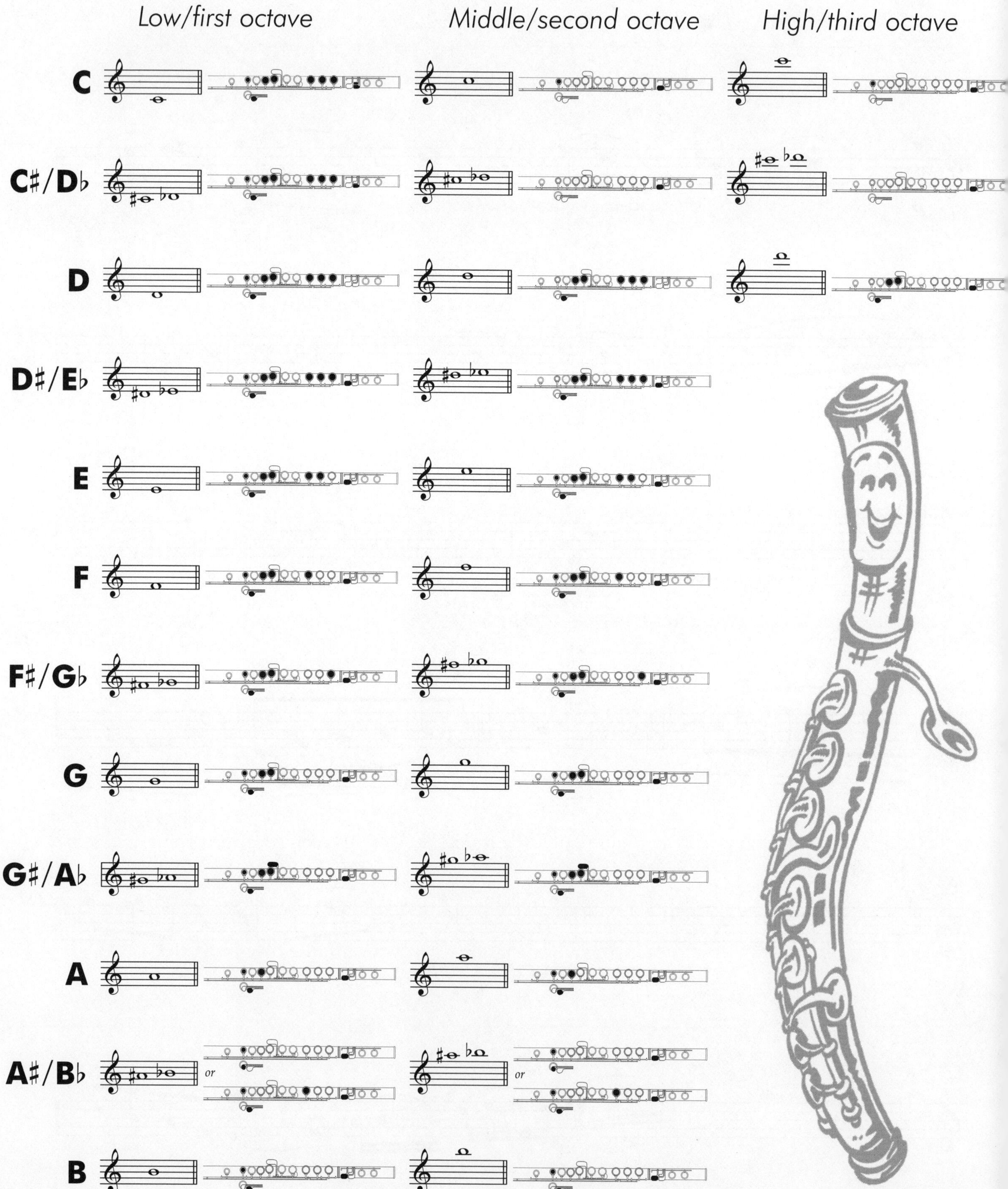
Low/first octave
Middle/second octave
High/third octave
C
C♯/D♭
D
D♯/E♭
E
F
F♯/G♭
G
G♯/A♭
A
A♯/B♭
or
or
B

THE FLUTE

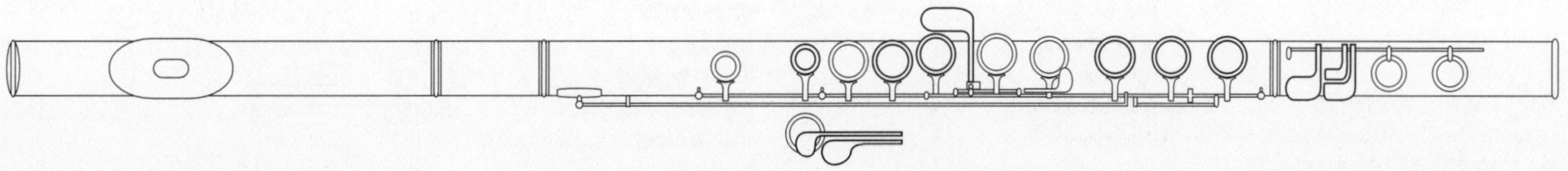

Putting it together

Your flute has three sections: the **head-joint**; the **body-joint** and the **foot-joint**.

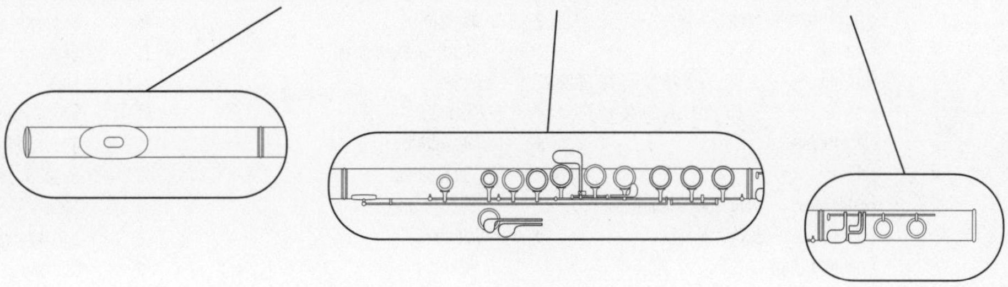

Always be *very* careful when you put your flute together – don't touch the keywork, as it will damage it.

- Take the head-joint out of the case and hold it in your left hand.
- Take out the body-joint and hold it around the barrel (where the writing is) and gently twist and push the two together.
- Line up the blow hole with the first key of the flute.
- Now hold the body with the left hand, and twist and push the foot-joint on without touching the keys.

Care of instrument

Always clean the insides of your flute after playing it.

- Take the flute apart to clean it, and never pull the rod all the way through the body-joint in case it gets stuck.
- Wipe the outside of the flute gently with a soft cloth or a silver polishing cloth.
- Always put the flute away after playing and make sure that you shut the case properly.

INDEX